Contract Law in the Czech Republic

Contract Law in the Czech Republic

Second Edition

Josef Fiala
Jan Hurdík

This book was originally published as a monograph in the International Encyclopaedia of Laws/Contracts.

Founding Editor: Roger Blanpain
General Editor: Frank Hendrickx
Volume Editor: Jacques Herbots

Wolters Kluwer

Published by:
Kluwer Law International B.V.
PO Box 316
2400 AH Alphen aan den Rijn
The Netherlands
E-mail: international-sales@wolterskluwer.com
Website: lrus.wolterskluwer.com

Sold and distributed in North, Central and South America by:
Wolters Kluwer Legal & Regulatory U.S.
7201 McKinney Circle
Frederick, MD 21704
United States of America
Email: customer.service@wolterskluwer.com

Sold and distributed in all other countries by:
Air Business Subscriptions
Rockwood House
Haywards Heath
West Sussex
RH16 3DH
United Kingdom
Email: international-customerservice@wolterskluwer.com

ISBN 978-94-035-2093-3

e-Book: ISBN 978-94-035-2165-7
web-PDF: ISBN 978-94-035-2131-2

The Authors

Prof. JUDr Josef Fiala, CSc, was born in Velké Mezirící near Brno, CR, in 1953, and graduated from Faculty of Law, J.E. Purkyne University (now Masaryk University), Brno, in 1979, becoming a full-time lecturer in the same year and subsequently an associate professor (docent) in 1995. Since 2005, he has been a professor. In addition to giving lectures, research and publication activities (as an author or a co-author, he has published over thirty books and about 200 articles and papers in journals and specialized publications), he has been engaged in a number of other activities related to legal practice. In 1992, he was an assistant to the Justice of the Constitutional Court of the Czechoslovak Federative Republic; since 1995, he has been an assistant and then counsellor to the Justice of the Constitutional Court of the Czech Republic; from 1998 to present he has been a member of the civil law committee of the Legislative Board of the Government of the Czech Republic, and he was also a member of the Civil Code recodification committee of the Ministry of Justice.

His dissertation on easement brought him in 1984 the degree of Candidate of Sciences (then an equivalent to PhD). In 1995, he took a higher doctorate (docent) with the work 'Ownership of Flats in the Czech Republic'. Currently, to the end of 2015, he has been the head of the Civil Law Department of the Faculty of Law, Masaryk University, in Brno. Since 2016, he is the judge of the Constitutional Court in Brno and continues his activities as the professor of Civil Law at the Faculty of Law, Masaryk University in Brno.

The Authors

Prof. JUDr Jan Hurdík, DrSc, was born in Trebíc, CR, in 1951, and graduated in 1976 from Faculty of Law, J.E. Purkyne University, Brno (now Masaryk University). He was a lecturer at the Department of History of State and Law in 1975–1976, an assistant and subsequently a public prosecutor at the public prosecutor's office in 1976–1980. In 1980, he became a member of the Civil Law Department of the Faculty of Law, Masaryk University, Brno, focusing mainly on civil law and private law jurisprudence as well as on civil procedure. In 1984, he obtained the degree of CSc. (then an equivalent to PhD) for his thesis 'Abuse of Civil Rights'. In 1995, he took a higher doctorate (docent) with his work 'Problems of Law of Foundations and Endowments'. In 2001, he was awarded the scientific degree of Doctor of Juristic Sciences (DrSc) by the Czech Academy of Sciences in Prague for his work 'Legal Persons – General Legal Characteristics'.

Since 2004, he has been a professor for civil law. He is an author and a co-author of fifty books and textbooks on various issues concerning civil law, and numerous articles and papers in specialized publications. In addition to that, he has been involved in a number of grant projects concerning research and university education in law, in the government committee preparatory works on the new Civil Code and, as the head, in a legislative committee preparing a law on foundations and endowments. Currently, he has been a head of the Civil Law Department of the Faculty of Law, Masaryk University, in Brno. He is a member of the scientific councils of the Faculty of Law of Masaryk University in Brno and the Faculty of Law of University in Plzeň. He is also a member of European Law Institute, SECOLA, and a former member of Acquis Group (2008–2012).

Table of Contents

The Authors 3

List of Abbreviations 11

Preface 13

General Introduction 15

§1. General Background of the Country 15

§2. Legal Family and the Czech Law 16

§3. Primacy of Legislation in the Czech Legal System 16

§4. The Position of the Judiciary 17

§5. Distinction Between Public Law and Private Law (Administrative Contracts) 17

§6. Distinction Between Civil Law and Commercial Law (Commercial Contracts) 18

Introduction to the Law of Contracts 21

§1. Definition of the Law of Contracts 21

§2. Historical Background of the Law of Contract 22

§3. Classification of Contracts 23

§4. Contracts and Torts 24

§5. Contract and Quasi-Contract 25

§6. Contracts and the Law of Property 26

§7. Contract and Trust 26

§8. Good Faith and Fair Dealing 26

§9. STYLE OF DRAFTING 27

§10. SOURCES OF THE LAW OF CONTRACT 28

Part I. General Principles of the Law of Contract 29

Chapter 1. Formation 29

§1. AGREEMENT AND *QUID PRO QUO* (RECIPROCITY) 29
I. Offer and Acceptance 29
II. Intention to Create Legal Relations 30
III. Consideration, Gratuitous Promises, Natural Obligations 32
A. Consideration 32
B. Gratuitous Promises 32
C. 'Natural Obligations' 33
IV. Modifications of the Contract 33

§2. FORMAL AND EVIDENCE REQUIREMENTS 36
I. Formal Requirements 36
A. Tender 37
B. Public Tender 37
C. Auction 37
II. Contract under Seal 37
III. 'Solemn' Contracts 37
IV. Evidence Requirement 38
V. Function of the Notary and Notarial Instruments 38
VI. Burden of Proof 39

§3. LIABILITY AND NEGOTIATIONS 40
I. Pre-contractual Liability 40
II. Breakdown of Negotiations 40
A. Termination 40

Chapter 2. Conditions of Substantive Validity 42

§1. ESSENTIAL ELEMENTS 42

Chapter 3. The Content of a Contract 50

§1. GENERAL EXPLANATION 50
I. Consequences 51
II. Grounds and Consequences of Invalidity 51

§2. INTERPRETATION 58

§3. CONDITIONAL CONTRACTS 59

Chapter 4. Privity of Contract 62

§1. The Rule of Privity of Contract 62
I. Third Parties and the Contract 62
II. Contract for the Benefit of a Third Party 62
III. Contract to the Debit of a Third Party 63

§2. Transfer of Contractual Rights and/or Obligations 63

§3. The Special Case of a Subcontract, for Example, the (Nominated) Subcontractor in Building Contracts 67

§4. *Actio Pauliana* 67

Chapter 5. Termination of a Contract 68

§1. Debt Fulfilment: Performance and Breach 68
I. Consequences of Performance 72
II. Breach of Contract 72

§2. Impossibility and Hardship: Unforeseen Impossibility 73

§3. Withdrawal from the Contract 74

§4. Setting-Off (Unilateral and by the Agreement) 75

§5. Agreement on Cancelling an Obligation 76

§6. Waiver of a Right 76

§7. Remission of Debt 76

§8. Renunciation 77

§9. By Lapse of Time 77

§10. Death of the Debtor or the Creditor 77

§11. Preclusion of Rights 77

§12. Debtor's Delay under 'Fixed' Contract 78

§13. Merger of Debts 78

Part II. Specific Contracts 79

Table of Contents

Chapter 1. Consumer Contract: General Provisions 80

§1. GENERAL RULES FOR CONSUMER CONTRACTS 80
I. Distance Contracts and Contracts Negotiated Outside Business Premises 81
II. Contracts Negotiated Outside Business Premises 83
III. Financial Services 83
IV. Timesharing Contracts 83

Chapter 2. Sales 84

§1. SALE OF MOVABLE THING 85

§2. SALE OF IMMOVABLE THING 87
I. Exchange (Barter) Contract 87
II. Sale of Goods in Shops 88
III. Sale (Transfer) of the Enterprise 89

Chapter 3. Contract for Work 91

Chapter 4. Healthcare 94

Chapter 5. Licences 96

Chapter 6. Loans 98

§1. LOAN FOR CONSUMPTION 98

§2. LOAN FOR USE 98

§3. CREDIT 99

§4. CONSUMER CREDIT 100

Chapter 7. Contract of Employment 101

Chapter 8. Lease Contracts 102

§1. GENERAL PROVISIONS 102

§2. LEASE OF FLATS AND HOUSES 103

§3. LEASE OF BUSINESS PREMISES (SPACE) 104

§4. LEASE OF A MEANS OF TRANSPORT (SPECIAL RULES) 104

§5. Accommodation 105

Chapter 9. Tenure (A Special Kind of Lease) 107

§1. Agricultural Tenure (Lease of a Land) 107

§2. Lease of an Enterprise 107

Chapter 10. Mandate Contracts 109

§1. Mandate 109

§2. Agency 110

§3. Undisclosed Mandate 111

§4. Forwarding/Shipping Agency 112

§5. Commercial Agency 113

Chapter 11. Bailment (Contract on Custody, Deposit) 116

§1. Bailment 116

§2. Custody of Securities 117

§3. Storage 117

Chapter 12. Transportation 120

§1. Transportation of Persons and Things 120
I. Transportation of Persons (Passengers) 120
II. Carriage of Goods 121

§2. Operating a Means of Transportation 123

Chapter 13. Obligations from Contract of Account, One-Time Deposit, Letter of Credit, and Collection 124

§1. Account 124

§2. One-Time Deposit 124

§3. Letter of Credit 124

§4. Collection 125

Chapter 14. Aleatory Obligations 126

§1. Insurance 126

§2. Wagering (Betting), Gaming and Drawing a Lot 130

Chapter 15. Civil Partnership 131

Chapter 16. Silent Partnership 133

Chapter 17. Private Annuity 135

Chapter 18. Retired Persons' Housing and Lodging 136

Chapter 19. Public Promises 137

Chapter 20. Promise of Compensation 138

Chapter 21. Package Tours (Travel Contract) 139

Chapter 22. Contract for Inspection Activities 141

Chapter 23. Quasi-Contracts 143

§1. Obligations Arising from Unjustified Enrichment 143
I. General Outline 143
II. The Obligations Arising from Unjustified Enrichment 143
III. Legal Consequences of Unjustified Enrichment 146

§2. Agency without Mandate (*Negotiorum Gestio*) and Using a Thing for the Benefit of Another Person 148

Selected Bibliography 151

Index 153

List of Abbreviations

al.	alinea (a clause within an article or within a § of a code or of a law – *see* par.)
and fol.	et sequential, et sequentes (and following)
Art.	article (also section; of a code or of a law – *see* §)
cf.	Compare
Coll.	Collection of Legal Acts of the Czech republic
e.g.	exempli gratia (for example)
etc.	et cetera (and so on)
i.e.	id est (that is)
para.	paragraph (a clause within an article or within a § of a code or of a law – *see* al.)
§	paragraph (of a code or of a law – *see* art.)

Preface

This book is a part of the encyclopaedia of law on contracts under the editorial project IEL outlining the system of contract law in the Czech Republic and reflecting the situation in the legislation as of 1 January 2014 by the end of August 2019. The work corresponds with the framework selected by the editor; however, it inevitably reacted to specific features of the law of contracts in the Czech Republic, which brought the need to adjust some of the parts of the publication as appropriate.

The current state of contract law in the Czech Republic has several specific features that should be pointed at. First of all, the sources of (internal) contract law in the Czech Republic were till 1 January 2014 composed of two most important acts of law: The Civil Code (Act No. 40, 1964 Coll.) and the Commercial Code (Act No. 513, 1991 Coll.). Both the codes contained specific rules for both commercial and non-commercial contracts and deeds but a strict dividing line between the two of them was often missing, and thus application of a particular rule of law to a given case is governed by rather complex rules.

Another feature influencing the character of the Czech contract law is its dynamic development following the fall of the Iron Curtain and the change of the political establishment after 1989 the law of contracts has, through a number of legislative changes including Commercial Code recodification, gradually returned to democratic standards of contract relationships, leaving aside the communist experiment in law, as applied between 1950 and 1989. However, a consistent change of the system of law necessarily meant the requirement of carrying out an entire recodification of private law as a whole, including the law of contract. Since 1992, legislative activities involving the entire recodification of the Czech private law have been in progress. The aim of the recodification was a large civil code, including family law. As for the basic types of contract, the new civil code should have contained all standard contract types including employment contracts and contracts used both in commercial relationships and beyond (which implies a commercialized concept of the civil code).

After twelve years of preparatory and legislative work, a set of laws representing the basis of recodification of private law in the Czech Republic was passed by the Czech Parliament:

- Act No. 89/2012 Coll., Civil Code;
- Act No. 90/2012 Coll. on Companies; and
- Act No. 91/2012 Coll. on Private International Law and Rules of Procedure.

Subsequently, a set of laws was passed forming an accompanying legislation making it possible to put the recodification into practice.

The acts representing the re-codified private law of the Czech Republic came into force on 1 January 2014.

Due to the above-mentioned reasons, this monograph is a substantially revised version of the previous monograph contract. The Czech Republic is providing an overview of the new Czech contract law which has become a part of the re-codified Civil Code. The authors are aware of the fact that it is one of the first treatments of the new contract law of the Czech Republic which will undoubtedly be changed in the future.

The authors respect the special terminology of the Czech contract law striving at the same time to adapt it to the language standards of the 'European' English.

The authors would like to thank PhDr Anna Lysá, CSc, Department of Legal Communication, Comenius University, Bratislava, Slovakia, for the translation of the original version of the work. The authors would also like to thank Prof. JUDr et PhDr. Michal Tomášek, DrSc., Faculty of Law, Charles University, Prague and Carissa Meyer, John Marshall Law School in Chicago, for corrections of the terminology, and especially Mgr. Radek Šimek, PhD, Faculty of Law, Masaryk University, Brno, Czech Republic for the final language correction of the text and for the translation of the updated text.

This monograph has been written with the support of Faculty of Law of Masaryk University in Brno.

General Introduction

§1. General Background of the Country

1. The Czech Republic is a unitary State created after the splitting of Czechoslovakia on 1 January 1993. The Constitution of the Czech Republic was adopted at the end of 1992, entering into force on 1 January 1993. The country is divided into fourteen regions. The capital of the country is Prague. Since 1 May 2004, the Czech Republic has been a Member State of the European Union (EU). The European law is in force in the Czech territory having supremacy over the Czech law.

The legislative power is exercised by the Parliament of the Czech Republic which consists of the Chamber of Deputies and the Senate. About 200 members of the Chamber of Deputies are elected in general and direct elections every four years. Eighty-one members of Senate are elected in general and direct elections for six years. The election takes place every two years in order to renew one-third of the Senate. Besides its legislative powers, the Parliament has also other important functions. The Chamber of Deputies must pass the annual State budget and the final account. The Senate gives its consent to the appointment of judges of the Constitutional Court. The head of the Czech Republic is the President of the Czech Republic elected directly by the citizens of the Czech Republic. The President of the Czech Republic can only be elected for two consecutive terms.

The executive power is partially vested in the Government of the Czech Republic and partially in the President of the Czech Republic. He is part of the executive power, too. He appoints the prime minister according to the result of the election to the Chamber of Deputies and appoints and dismisses each Minister of the Government on the proposal of the prime minister. The primary task of the government consists of issuing regulations and making decisions needed for implementation of laws.

The judiciary power is independent of the executive and legislative powers. The Constitutional Court has the authority to pass judgments on constitutionality of laws enacted by the legislature and on regulations enacted by the executive authorities. The ordinary law courts are organized in four degrees – district courts, regional or municipal courts, high courts and Supreme Court. Administrative courts have jurisdiction over public law controversies outside constitutional issues, in particular over challenges to administrative acts.

§2. Legal Family and the Czech Law

2. A legal culture has been in the territory of what is now the Czech Republic from time immemorial. As early as the thirteenth century, land records, the legal registers of noble estates existed in Bohemia. At the beginning of the fourteenth century, under reign of the Czech King Wenceslas II, Roman law was partially adopted (*ius regale montanorum*). From 1620 to 1918, the Czech legal system developed within the framework of the Austrian empire. At the beginning of twentieth century, the German Civil Code (BGB) influenced the development of the Austrian legal system, including the Czech one. Some elements of the French legal system penetrated to the Czech law after the establishment of the Czechoslovak Republic in 1918. Particularly the constitutional system of the Czechoslovak Republic adopted some elements of the French Constitution of the Third Republic. The general system of private law remained untouched until 1950 when the Czechoslovak law was subject to the influence of the Soviet legal system. Under the communist regime (1950–1989), the democratic principles of civil law were distorted. After 1989, the Czech legal system finds again its original roots but some of its new codifications are more and more inspired by modern European codifications, particularly of the German origin.

The new Civil Code, effective from 1 January 2014, even if inspired by various sources, draws heavily on the non-realized draft of the 1938 Czechoslovak Civil Code which was a modernized version of the Austrian ABGB from 1811.

§3. Primacy of Legislation in the Czech Legal System

3. In the Czech Republic, lawmaking must proceed by means of legislation. There is therefore no customary law as such. Customs can be considered only in those cases in which a statue refers to them.

Other important sources of law are international treaties and international covenants of human rights. Those international treaties and covenants have a direct binding effect and supremacy over statutes. The Czech Republic as an EU Member State is also bound by the EU law concerning protection of human rights.

The Constitution takes precedence over statutes. The priority of the Constitution is especially important with respect to provisions protecting fundamental individual rights. All ordinary statutes are void or may be declared void insofar as they violate any fundamental constitutional rights. The priority of statutory law over administrative regulations results from the subordinate position of the administrative agencies with respect to the legislature. Furthermore, an administrative agency may promulgate legal norms only on the basis of a formal statutory delegation of power which specifies the content, purpose and scope of the authority so granted. Duties and obligations can be imposed only by statutes, not by administrative provisions.

Two rules govern the conflict between legal norms otherwise having the same priority: a recent law prevails over a prior law; specific norms prevail over the more general ones. The mutual conflict of the principles (which are one of the sources of the Czech law) is solved on the basis of the so-called proportionality test.

§4. The Position of the Judiciary

4. Court decisions and writings were not until 1 January 2014 considered to be sources of law; nevertheless, they often had a decisive influence upon courts and administrative authorities. In this context, rules of interpretation are of great importance, such as interpretation of words, grammatical-logical interpretation, interpretation of intention analogy of statute, analogy of legal principle or principles of natural law.

In order to guarantee a uniform case law, only the Supreme Court and the Supreme Administrative Court can give their opinions to unification of the case law. Such opinions do not have nature of a generally binding source of law. However, in practice, they are followed by all courts. With the adoption of the new Civil Code, the position of judicial decisions was emphasized in the court practice: pursuant to section 13, C.C., courts are bound to follow the judicial decision made in a similar case; a different decision must be convincingly reasoned.

A special position is granted to the Constitutional Court. The Constitutional Court may declare void any statute or its provisions insofar as they violate the Constitution or an international treaty having supremacy over the Czech law. The Constitutional Court may declare void any administrative regulation or its provisions insofar as they violate the Constitution or an international treaty having supremacy over the Czech law. The decisions of the Constitutional Court are the so-called negative source of law. The Constitutional Court is not a lawmaking authority, but it can declare void the existing sources of law or their parts.

§5. Distinction Between Public Law and Private Law (Administrative Contracts)

5. Until 1950, civil or private law was understood as all that was not public law; thus, it included even commercial law. Legal writers for some time used the term 'private law' in a narrower sense excluding commercial law. However, between 1950 and 1989, the distinction between 'private' and 'public' law was considered inappropriate. After 1989, a new discussion on this topic was opened. An important step towards solving the problem of distinction between private and public law was establishing necessary criteria of such a distinction. The first one of them may be criteria of involvement and the second one may be criteria of power.

According to the criteria of involvement, private law respects freedom of an individual while public law protects public interests and the public order. Such classification is dating back to Roman law as expressed by Ulpianus: *Publicum ius est, quod ad statum rei romanae spectat; privatum, quod ad singulorum utilitatem.* According to the criteria of power, public law expresses the dominant position of the State authority in protecting public interests and the public order. The Czech legislators accepted the dualism of public and private law again after 1991 in several modifications of the Civil Code. A renewal of dualism of private and public law in the Czech legal system was regarded as an instrument of reinforcing legal guarantees of the natural or artificial legal persons and preventing the State from unauthorized interventions in private business activities.

6. The new Czech Civil Code is based on the primary principle of private autonomy to which the principle of equality of the parties is subordinated.

The principle of equality is undoubtedly one of the basic principles of legal regulation of private law. The public authority can influence private law relationships or create their inequality under limited and special conditions:

– A particular interest to protect special categories of civil law relationships, for example, protection of children or protection of persons who are not capable to defend effectively their own interests.
– Protection of some participants of a civil law relationship against economic supremacy of other participants which could lead, respecting formal equality of the participants, to a devaluation of the social purpose of the legal relationship, for example, consumer protection, abuse of the dominant position, etc.

7. Due to the distinction between private and public law, the contract law is influenced in the same way. Apart from typical private law contracts concluded between parties with a private law status, there are contracts concluded within a public law regulatory framework (administrative contracts):

(a) Between public authorities, for example, communities, states, or its regions. These administrative contracts are concluded in the situations when statutes do not directly establish a subordinate position between the persons in question. In such cases, norms of private law are applied to administrative contracts.
(b) Administrative contracts can also be applied as a part of public law relationships created between public authorities and private individuals. In such cases, administrative contracts can partially reflect contractual autonomy of participants. For example, a decision on a subsidy granted by public authority to a private individual can be accompanied by an administrative contract providing for concrete conditions of such a subsidy, etc.

§6. Distinction Between Civil Law and Commercial Law (Commercial Contracts)

8. As mentioned above, the Czechoslovak legal system in 1950–1989 did not make any distinction between private law and public law. Thus, no discussion was possible on the broader sense of private law or on its narrower sense excluding commercial law. Starting from 1948, an extensive State control and central planning of the economy were introduced, and in 1964 the Economic Code more or less established an administrative regulation of economic contracts. Those were more similar to the above-described administrative contracts than to commercial contracts in the sense of continental legal systems.

After 1989, the concept of 'private law' was renewed in Czechoslovakia but in a very broad sense including commercial law as well, as a reaction to its previous absence in our legal system. Amendments to the Civil Code in 1991 and the introduction of a new Commercial Code in 1991 created a dual codification of private law. The Civil Code represented a general codification of private law including contract law, while the Commercial Code was a special codification for commercial contracts and for persons of commercial relationships such as commercial companies and cooperative companies.

The new Czech Civil Code put private and commercial contract law together into one code and abolished the existing Commercial Code. From the existing Commercial Code it incorporated the second part, that is, the law of companies, into the separate Act No. 90/2012 Coll. on Companies, and the third part, that is, commercial obligations, was unified in the fourth part of the new Civil Code.

The text of the Civil Code contains, nevertheless, a few of the special rules, applicable only to the commercial contracts. Some Czech scholars arrange the commercial rules (as the subsystem of private law, belonging to the 'special private laws') among the family law, labour law, consumer law, etc.

Introduction to the Law of Contracts

§1. Definition of the Law of Contracts

9. In the Czech legal system, contract law is a part of the law of obligations. It is a part of broader private law, comprising a set of legal rules on contracts (obligations). The central term of contract law is an obligation by which the following is usually understood:

- the obligation as legal relationship (obligation in a broader sense);
- the obligation arising from this legal relationship (obligation in a narrower sense).

Other fundamental terms of contract law are:

- claim and debt;
- creditor and debtor.

Under the contract law, a claim is a subjective right of one party (creditor) to the contract relationship to demand from the other party of the same relationship (debtor) certain performance, that is, demand from him/her to give something, to act or to refrain from acting, that is, omitting. If the claim becomes payable (mature) it principally becomes a title, that is, unless a voluntary performance was provided by the debtor, it may be successfully claimed in a court or in an arbitral tribunal. The debt (obligation in a narrower sense) is a corresponding obligation (a duty) of a party to the contract (the debtor) to provide the other party to the same obligation relationship, the creditor, with the performance demanded by him/her and promised by the debtor in consistency with the claim. The creditor is generally the party to the contract who has a claim (rights), the debtor is the party who has a duty (obligation) to satisfy such a claim.

Binding legal relationships arising from contracts may be classified according to the branches of private law into civil contract law including now commercial contracts and possibly also into contract law of other branches (e.g., labour contract law). From another point of view, contract law distinguishes between general contract law and specific contract law. Further, binding legal relationships were historically classified according to its source of formation: obligations relationship arising from contracts, or from quasi-contracts and obligations enforceable from torts, or from quasi-torts.

The most frequent and typical ground for formation of an obligation relationship is a contract. It is habitual to distinguish between provisions on obligations arising from contracts and also provisions on some quasi-contracts, for example, benevolent intervention in another's affairs (acting for another's benefit without agency, *negotiorum gestio*), public promise and public tender. Contract is a fundamental notion of contract law. It is a bilateral or a multilateral agreement which gives rise to a binding legal relationship or which has some other legal effect. Contract is composed of two or more unilateral juridical acts.

§2. Historical Background of the Law of Contract

10. During the eighteenth century, a general codification of private law was planned in order to rectify the fragmentation that had existed to that time. In 1753, the Empress Maria Theresia appointed a commission to compile the existing law and to fill in the gaps according to 'right reason'. The resulting *Codex Theresianus* of 1866 was, however, not adopted due to its casuistic and voluminous nature. A later reworking of this code was enacted under the Emperor Joseph II in 1787 as the *Josephinisches Gesetzbuch*. On 1 June 1811, the Civil Code ABGB (*Allgemeines Bürgerliches Gesetzbuch*) was proclaimed, entering into force on 1 January 1812. The code was based predominantly on Roman law, and in part on German law, and was strongly influenced by the natural law doctrine. The ABGB applied in all territories that belonged to the Austrian half of the Empire, including the Czech lands – Bohemia, Moravia and the southern part of Silesia. The Commercial Code was adopted in 1863 and the Civil Procedure Code in 1895.

The development of the BGB in 1896 brought about a revision of the already 100-year-old ABGB. In three revisions (1914, 1915 and 1916), the ABGB was in part newly organized according to the model of BGB. When the independent Czechoslovak State came into existence in 1918, the new Czechoslovak Republic continued to apply these generally valid codes in the Czech lands. In Slovakia, Hungarian law was applied in the sphere of civil law. From the very beginning of the independent Czechoslovak State, work on the new Czechoslovak Civil Code was started. The draft was ready in 1938, but due to the Nazi occupation and to the post-war development in Czechoslovakia, it never entered into force.

After the liberation of the Republic in 1945 and particularly after the communist takeover in 1948, the former legal system gradually underwent radical changes as a result of the transformation which occurred in the whole social and economic system. A new Civil Code was adopted in 1950 (No. 141, 1950 Col.) which replaced the ancient Civil Code from 1811

The new Civil Code adopted in 1964 (No. 40, 1964 Col.) was strongly influenced by the contemporary political trends. It was based on the theory that 'civil law regulated only the economic relationships arising among socialist organizations and citizens and among citizens in the process of satisfying their own needs'. The rest of private law was divided into several branches each of them with a special codification – family law (Family Act No. 94, 1963 Col.), labour law (Labour Code No. 65, 1965 Col.), economic (commercial) law (Economic Code No. 109/1964 Col.) and private international law (Private International Law Act No. 97/1963 Col.). In the period of 1964–1989, it was impossible to apply the Czechoslovak Civil Code to international trade due to its strong political orientation. Therefore, in

Czechoslovakia there existed at that time in fact two Civil Codes – the 'internal' Civil Code (No. 40/1964 Col.) and the 'Civil Code for international trade' – International Trade Code No. 101/1963 Col. the Economic Code No. 109/1964 Col. was applied to 'internal' economic contracts, that is, to 'contacts among the socialist organizations'.

11. After 1989, when Czechoslovakia was re-establishing its democratic order and the rule of law, it became necessary to rebuild its legal system as a whole. Already in 1989 and 1990, the Constitution was substantially amended, in particular as regards democratization of the society and basic freedoms in personal and property relationships. The first stage of the reconstruction of private law meant substantial amendments to the Civil Code. The International Trade Code was abolished; the Family Act and the Labour Code were amended. The Economic Code was abolished as well, and commercial law was restored in the country with a new Commercial Code No. 513/1991 Col.

In the 1990s, in particular after the split of Czechoslovakia in 1993, the development of private law was oriented on two matters: to prepare the accession of the Czech Republic to the EU with regard to the necessary approximation of legislations and to make a general reform of the Czech private law in compliance with modern needs. The first task was accomplished by the date of accession of the country to the EU on 1 May 2004. The second one, the general reform of the Czech private law already went through its principal stage, and a draft of the new Civil Code has actually been accomplished. The bill on the new Civil Code was approved by the Parliament of Czech Republic in 2012, being signed by the President of the Czech Republic and coming into force on 1 January 2014. It has become the dominant and general source of private law with links to special legislation in different areas of private law, particularly the Labour Code (a new Labour Code was adopted – No. 262/2006 Col.). Codification of international private law was realized by the same date (No 91/2012 Col.) being in force from 1 January 2014.

From the passing of the Civil Code (2012), some amendments of the Civil Code were made, but the part of contractual obligations was not changed.

§3. Classification of Contracts

12. Classification of contracts is based on the same criteria as classification of any other juridical acts:

(1) According to the number of parties – bilateral or multilateral contracts.
(2) According to the value of the transaction – reciprocal or gratuitous.
(3) According to the form – formal or informal.
(4) According to the subject matter, we recognize:
   - contracts with monetary performance where at least one party's performance is provided in money;
   - contracts with non-monetary performance.

Particular contract types may be classified as follows:

(1) Contracts creating an obligation relationship – typical, 'named' contracts (as described in the Civil Code) or atypical, 'unnamed' contracts (not explicitly described in the codes) or mixed contracts (paragraph 1746 Civil Code).[1]
(2) Concluding unnamed or mixed contracts by parties is based on their freedom to contract; however, they must not be inconsistent with mandatory rules of law, good morals, public order and/or with rules regarding protection of persons.
(3) Contracts to guarantee obligation relationship.
(4) Contracts causing change in an obligation relationship (e.g., contract on assignment).
(5) Contracts causing termination of an obligation relationship (e.g., agreement on setting-off).

§4. Contracts and Torts

13. Obligations as relationships may also be created by unlawful acts – torts. In the former Czech Civil Code[2] contractual and delictual liability was not distinguished, so the rule of non-cumul was not needed. The Czech civil law has returned since 2014 to distinguishing the legal constructions of contractual and delictual liability.

The rule of non-cumul is not expressly incorporated into the current Civil Code, Nevertheless, the court practice does not accept a cumulative compensation for one damage being provided 'twice'. The Czech civil law does not exclude claiming compensation for damage partially as contractual and partially as delictual right:[3]

(a) Liability arising from the breach of statutory rule(s) is divided into two essential groups:
    (1) The general concept of this liability requires the following conditions: (i) Breach of a statute;[4] (ii) the breach must either (ba) interfere with an absolute right of the injured person, or (bb) interfere with another right of the injured person by a breach of a statutory duty aimed at protection of such a right; (iii) the third condition is fault in form of negligence. Negligence is presumed if the tortfeasor acts in a manner different from what can be reasonably expected from a person in his position. Negligence is also

1. See Decision of the Supreme Court from 14.06.2016, 32 Cdo 1698/2016
2. Act No. 40/1964 Coll.
3. There is, nevertheless, one exception: as the Czech civil law allows claiming remedies based on the faulty performance arising out of a contract obligation, the contractual party is not allowed to replace that type of claim by a financial compensation for the damage: See the text of Section (§) 1925 Civil Code:

    A right from a defective performance does not exclude the right to compensation for damage; however, what can be achieved by asserting the right from a defective performance may not be claimed for any other legal cause.

4. For more details see Section (§) 6 Civil Code.

presumed if the tortfeasor declared to have special knowledge, skill or diligence, or such a knowledge, skill or diligence is required for his performance. The tortfeasor is entitled to exculpating himself if he proves that he did not know or could not know about the danger of his behaviour leading to the harm.

(2) The Czech legislator uses in the group of special cases the concept of strict (objective) liability. There are special situations where the situation itself requires compensation of the harm arisen. This type of legal responsibility is also called liability for the result.

(b) The breach of contractual duty brings about the duty for the contractual party in breach to provide compensation for the resulting damage. The entitled person is mainly the other contractual party but it can also be the person whose interest has been interfered with through the breach of the contractual duty.

The contractual responsibility for injury is built on the basis of strict, i.e., objective, liability. It means that the tortfeasor is not able/allowed to exculpate himself if he provides a proof consisting in absence of his fault. The tortfeasor is only entitled to relieve (liberate) himself if he proves that he was temporarily or permanently prevented from fulfilling his contractual duty due to an extraordinary, unforeseeable and insurmountable obstacle created independently of his will. The Czech judiciary and civil commentaries call the above-mentioned reasons of liberation vis maior.[5] In addition to the breach of contractual duty, the contractual responsibility for injury also requires the foreseeability of the injury that can occur.[6]

§5. CONTRACT AND QUASI-CONTRACT

14. The new Czech Civil Code did not fully accept the Roman classification of the sources of obligation in *contractus, quasi-contractus, delictus, quasi-delictus*. The Czech Civil Code states explicitly (paragraph 1722) that all obligations arise from contracts as well as from unlawful acts or other facts laid down by the law. In the Czech law, a great majority of obligations in practice are created by contracts (*ex contractu*). There are, however, some unilateral juridical acts which could create an obligation. Such obligations, similar to obligations created by contracts, are called quasi-contracts. The C.C. describes agency without mandate (*negotiorum gestio)* and using someone else's thing for the benefit of someone else, public tender, public promise and some others.

The Czech Civil Code contains provisions on some other sources of obligations, namely unjustified enrichment as well as *obligatio quasi ex delicto*.

5. See Hulmák a kol., Občanský zákoník VI. Závazkové právo. Zvláštní část (§§ 2055–3014). Komentář. 1. vydání. Praha: Nakladatelství C. H. Beck, 2014, p. 1574.
6. Dobešová, Lenka & Hurdík, Jan. 'Czech Republic'. In International Encyclopaedia of Laws: Tort Law, edited by Britt Weyts. Alphen aan den Rijn, NL: Kluwer Law International, 2017. Marg. No. 20-23

§6. Contracts and the Law of Property

15. We can find in the Czech law a distinction between absolute rights and relative rights. An absolute right is a right to property that can be upheld against everyone. A relative right is connected with a person (all rights to the performance of an obligation are relative rights).

Absolute rights are right to property (ownership), copyright, patent, etc. There is a closed system of real rights whereas the system of obligations is open.

A majority of private law contracts are obligation contracts, that is, contracts leading to the formation, a change or the termination of a contractual obligation relationship. There are, however, contracts leading to the formation, a change or the extinction of real rights.

These are exceptional under the Czech law, as a result of the two-phase construction adopted for obtaining ownership (or the formation of another real right), namely in relation to real property. The first stage means the formation of a contract; the second stage is registration of such a contract by a State authority – Land Register.

§7. Contract and Trust

16. The trust as a specific legal conception was not known in the Czech law. There are some cases of legal relationships on the basis of which a person – owner of a certain property – was under a contractual duty to manage and administer this property on behalf of someone else. An example can be the Czech Organization of Copyright administering copyright on behalf of authors.

As of 1 January 2014, the concept of trust was introduced into the Czech private law in the form of a special fund being without legal personality which may be entrusted with administration of another person's property. The property entrusted to the trust becomes independent from the existing owner and has its own regime. This type of trust is a breakthrough into the principle of non-existence of property without an owner.

The trusts, newly introduced into the Czech law, evoked the discussion among the lawyers. A number of authors criticize its ability to become an instrument of abusive practices. On that account, the legal regulation of trusts was subsequently tightened.

§8. Good Faith and Fair Dealing

17. As stated above, the Czech civil law is governed by three equity principles of contract law:

> Contracts must not be contrary to good morals (contra bonos mores). The term 'good morals' is commonly interpreted as a set of moral rules applied together

with the formal legal norms. The contracts that are contrary to good morals are void, that is, they are deemed to be concluded but without any legal consequences.

The term 'good faith' (bona fides) is applied under Czech law either as a general principle or a prerequisite of fairness in the conduct of parties to contracts or as a psychological category, expressing the psychological state in which the party to contract is not aware of legal errors related to the contract. In the latter sense, good faith applies when expressly referred to by law.

The new Civil Code did not adopt the concepts of Good Faith and Fair Dealing substituting them in a similar meaning with concepts such as Good Moral, Fairness and some other equivalents.

§9. Style of Drafting

18. The law of contract is based on some general principles of which the central one is equality of parties in consumer contracts modified by protection of the weaker contractual party. But the primary principle is that of freedom to contract as an expression of autonomy of will. It is expressed, for example, in Article 2, al. 3 of the Czech Charter of Fundamental Rights and Freedoms which stipulates that 'everyone is authorized to do anything what is not prohibited by law'.

Freedom to contract means predominantly the freedom to conclude or not to conclude a contract, to select a contractual party, the type of contract, to determine the content of the contract or the content of obligation relationship to be formed by a contract, to denote the form of the contract and finally to refrain from a contract under stated conditions:

(a) Freedom to contract – Party autonomy may be restricted by law only through imposing a duty to conclude a contract, for example, a contract on energy supply, on public transport, on radio and television broadcasting. Certain restrictions of freedom to contract may also arise from voluntary contracts (e.g., *pactum de contrahendo*).
(b) Free choice of the contractual party may be excluded due to public interests (e.g., regulation on sale or providing of some goods or services as well as electricity, gas and water.).
(c) Contractual parties may agree on other types of contracts, different from those stipulated by law; there is no numerous clauses, a limited number of contracts allowed (cf. options for atypical contracts – §1746).
(d) Freedom to contract – Party autonomy is established by mandatory rules of law that may not be excluded or diverted from by the parties in contracting. Mandatory rules are not very frequent; at present, they serve to protect the weaker party of the contract (e.g., consumer protection – *see*, e.g., the provision of general consumer contracts or the particular provisions on liability for faulty goods sold in shops).

(e) Contractual parties can conclude contracts in any form – explicitly (in oral or in written form) or in another way which does not give rise to doubts on what the party wished to express; unless certain formalities have not been stipulated by statute or agreed by the parties.

§10. Sources of the Law of Contract

19. Law of contract is a part of private law. Legal regulation of contract law may be found in several statutes:

(a) The basic contract law regulations of the general nature are laid down in the Civil Code, now Act No. 89/2012 Coll., Civil Code. Part I, Chapter V, regulates various legal concepts including limitation. A complex regulation of contract law can be found in the fourth part of the C.C. which also regulates obligations arising from delicts and other binding reasons.

(b) Further legal rules contain provisions on some specific kinds of obligations not regulated in the codes mentioned. These are, for example:
   - Act No. 121/2000 Coll. on copyright, the related rights and on some other acts of law as amended (Copyright Act).
   - Act No. 527/1990 Coll. on inventions, industrial designs and innovations.
   - Act No. 207/2000 Coll. on industrial designs protection.
   - Act No. 262/2006 Coll., Labour Code.
   - Act No. 257/2016 Coll., on Consumer Credit.

Part I. General Principles of the Law of Contract

Chapter 1. Formation

§1. Agreement and *Quid Pro Quo* (Reciprocity)

I. Offer and Acceptance

20. Under the Czech law, contracts are bilateral or multilateral juridical acts arising from bilateral or multilateral manifestation of will. Such expressions of will should be of identical content and should express mutual assent.

One of the juridical acts is a proposal to conclude a contract – an offer. Offer is an expression of will, by which the offeror proposes the offeree to conclude a contract on the subject matter given in the offer. The offer contains two elements: the first one concerns the contractual assent, the second one is about the determination of the content of the future contract. The offer is effective from the time it has been delivered to the offeree.

The offer is irrevocable:

- if irrevocability is expressed in it;
- if the parties have agreed so;
- if it results from the negotiation of the parties about concluding the contract, from their previous business contact or from custom.

The offer, even though it is irrevocable, may be cancelled by the offeror, if the cancellation reaches the offeree before the offer has been served on him/her or at the same time with the service of the offer.

The offer even if revocable, may not be revoked:

- within the time limit stated for its acceptance, unless the right to revoke prior to the expiry of that time is implied in the offer;
- if irrevocability is stipulated in the offer.

A revocable offer may be revoked by the offeror if the revocation reaches the offeree before the offeree has dispatched an acceptance.

The offer is binding for the offeror, although not for an indefinite time. First, the time limit stated by the offeror for the acceptance of the offer must be considered. An offer may not be revoked for the reasons just stated. But an offer irrevocable expires:

- by the expiry of the time stated for the acceptance;
- by the expiry of a reasonable time, taking into account the nature of the contract proposed and communication means used by the offeror for dispatching the offer;
- by delivering the offeree's rejection of the offer to the offeror.

Unless accepted immediately, an oral offer or a written offer between the present persons is terminated if not stated otherwise in the offer.

The second juridical act is the acceptance. Accepting an offer, the offeree manifests his/her will to the offeror to accept his/her offer and concludes a contract with him/her on the subject matter as stated in the offer. The acceptance may be carried out by a declaration or a conduct by the offeree (e.g., by performance). In any case, it must be a manifestation of will carried out on time. The acceptance becomes effective the moment the consent with the expressed offer reaches the offeror. A conveyance contract does not require any prompt declaration of acceptance by the offeree; a written declaration in the same document containing the offer is sufficient. The acceptance of an offer made to the absent offeror is effective only after the reply of the offeree reaches the offeror.

The acceptance may be revoked if the respective revocation has reached the offeror sooner than or simultaneously with the acceptance. A late acceptance is nonetheless effective as the acceptance if, without undue delay, the offeror at least orally informs the offeree that it is treated as an effective acceptance. However, an answer expressing the acceptance but containing supplements, reservations, restrictions, or other changes (modified acceptance) is a rejection of the offer, and it is deemed to be a new offer (counteroffer). Above-mentioned does not apply to the answer containing complements or divergents that do not substantially change the terms of the offer; it is an acceptance of the offer if the offeror does not refuse it without necessary delay. The offeror may exclude the acceptance of such an offer in advance.

The moment of conclusion of a contract is described by section 1745 Civil Code, under which a contract has been concluded at the moment the acceptance of the offer has become effective. Silence or inaction in itself does not *eo ipso* imply the acceptance.

II. Intention to Create Legal Relations

21. Offer and acceptance are juridical acts, that is, manifestations of will to conclude a contract. Thus, an offer and acceptance must contain:

(a) manifestation of will;
(b) declaration of the extent of the manifestation of will to conclude a contract with the recipient of the offer;
(c) recognition of the manifestation of will by the rules of law;

(d) consequences following the intention expressed by the manifestation of will.

(a) Manifestation of will is an essential concept, implying unity of two components: will and manifestation.

The will is an element of a juridical act together with awareness of legal consequences of the acting person as the subjective aspect of the manifestation of will. The will designates a mental category and expresses an inner mental relation of the acting person to the intended legal consequences. As a result, the will must understand the significance of a juridical act created in a qualified manner. The requirement that the will should be manifested in a certain way recognized by law denies or reduces legal relevance of the will of such persons who, due to the lack of mental capacity or maturity, are unable to properly predict the consequences of their will manifestation. Therefore, the manifestation of will made by a person incapable of rational decision-making due to his/her lack of mental capacity or his/her age has no legal effect.

The will may be manifested in any manner enabling recognition of its content. According to manifestation of will, we can distinguish:

- an explicit manifestation;
- an implicit manifestation.

An explicit manifestation can be performed orally, in writing or by sign language. With regard to increasing use of modern methods of recording, processing and transferring of information, using of agreed or usual codes, signs, etc., is possible as well. For some juridical acts, a certain manner of explicit manifestation is prescribed (e.g., a written form of a contract concerning real estate). Implicit manifestation of will is a manifestation communicated in other than an express manner, for example, by acting (tearing the testament, etc.) or by omission (expressing the will not to make the contract by inaction of the offeree in reaction to the offer). Omissions are legally relevant only if it is inaction or silence in situations where acting is necessary.

Generally, one may act legally by conduct or omission; it may occur expressly or in another way which does not provoke a doubt about what the acting person wanted to express.

(b) The requirement to declare the extent of manifestation of will means that the will must be intended to result in the rise, a change or the termination of legal relation (rights and obligations).

Various views within the civil law theory have been expressed involving the extent of will to cause legal consequences. The prevailing and most logical concept is that manifestation need not comprise all legal consequences of an act. It is not possible for a layperson (non-professional) to comprise by his/her will all detailed legal consequences that may be attached to his/her will by legal rules. Therefore, a will of a person, including essential consequences, is sufficient. Further consequences will necessarily arise under law if determined by cogent rules (conditioned by non-mandatory provisions unless excluded by the parties as agreed). Therefore, a person need not be clearly and entirely aware of all legal consequences; it is sufficient if he/she intends certain (fundamental) legal consequences to arise.

From the previously stated, it follows *a contrario* that where there is no will to create legal consequences there is no juridical act. Acts of social service are not juridical acts for the same reason. For example, to refrain from smoking in places where smoking is not prohibited by law is not of legal nature; therefore, such a manifestation of will is not intended to create legal consequences.

(c) Manifestation of will gives rise to legal consequences only if such a manifestation of will is recognized by law (approved). Therefore, recognition of will by legal rules is another concept of juridical acts. If this concept is missing, the manifestation of will is not deemed relevant under law. Pursuant to the new Civil Code, the legal conduct must conform to good manners as well as laws in its content and purpose.

(d) For a juridical act, it is not sufficient that manifestation of will is recognized by rules of law, but certain legal consequences must be attached to it by law.

Moreover, it is stated under (b) that these consequences are those intended to arise by the acting person (if concerning fundamental consequences). In other acts, for example, in illegal acts as well as in persons' behaviour that is not determined by will but that is subject to law, consequences also arise, however, not by the will of the acting person but by force of law.

III. Consideration, Gratuitous Promises, Natural Obligations

A. *Consideration*

22. The Czech law does not know the doctrine of consideration as it is known in the common law system.

B. *Gratuitous Promises*

23. Gratuitous promises to perform something exist in the Czech legal system as exceptions, the standard form of such promises being a deed of donation, public promise and promise of indemnity.

Unilateral contracts attach the debtor's position to one party only and the creditor's position to another party. Apart from all subsidiary rights and obligations of the debtor and the creditor, for example, a duty to provide cooperation in performance and right to cooperation to be provided, the subject matter of the contract will be one performance only. An example, and in fact an exception to value relations governed by civil law of contracts, is the obligation established by a gift covenant (deed of donation).

Another type of a gratuitous contract under Czech law is public promise and promise of indemnity/compensation (*see* Part II, Chapters 19 and 20).

A special position in contract law is held by a mental reservation. It is a belief of a party to the contract that in relation to concluding a contract another advantage will be granted; this belief, however, is not expressed towards the other party in a significant manner. This mental reservation is not legally binding under Czech law and is not a part of contracts.

C. *'Natural Obligations'*

24. The Czech civil law distinguishes a subjective right, that is, the ability of a person to behave in a legal way, and a claim, that is, the property law based on its enforceability by the State power, exceptionally exercised by an authorized person.

The claim thus comprises the following:

(a) presents enforceability of a subjective right against the will of the obliged person;
(b) its existence is linked to a subjective right;
(c) presents an option to use State power or self-help for the claim enforcement.

In most instances the Czech law of contract provides subjective rights through claim, an exception being a group of the natural obligations. These are rights that cannot be enforced by court or by an authorized person. These include rights that are subject to period of limitation, rights from wagering, games and lotteries that are not officially permitted or are not organized by the State and rights arising from loans for such wagering and games (sections 2874, 2877, 2881–2883 Civil Code).

Civil law recognizes as exceptions such obligations that the legislator refuses to provide with enforceability through State or personal enforcement, that is, obligations that do not constitute a claim. It is in fact the type of incomplete rules (*lex imperfecta*) that are denoted as natural obligations (*obligationes naturales*) under contract law. These obligations are characterized by the following features:

- lack of the ability to demand performance by enforcement – performance may be exercised only through a voluntary act of the debtor;
- if performance was exercised in this manner, its return cannot be demanded under the stipulation on unjust enrichment;
- obligations arising from loans in wagering, games and lotteries;
- obligations for which the period of limitation (prescription) has expired;
- obligations invalid due to lack of formalities (paragraph 2997 C.C.).

IV. Modifications of the Contract

25. The Czech civil law recognizes the following changes in the content and the subject matter:

(a) agreement on modification (*cumulative novation*);
(b) settlement (*transactio*);
(c) debtor's delay (*mora debitoris*);
(d) creditor's delay (*mora creditoris*).

(a) Agreement of the Parties (Cumulative Novation)

26. With regard to the principle *pacta sunt servanda*, the parties may, by agreement, modify their mutual rights and obligations. In fact, the parties conclude a new contract in order to modify the former one.

Cumulative novation, as a form of an obligation relationship change, may be considered an instance in which the parties agree on a new obligation that will substitute the current obligation.

Securing rights of the respective novations continues but is limited by protection of third persons.

(b) Settlement

27. The current obligation can also be replaced in such a manner that the parties settle their mutual rights and obligation, so far questionable, by an agreement.

If the settlement concerns a right in rem recorded in a public register, the effects of such a settlement arise by recording it into this register.

This agreement, also called *transactio*, is aimed to make up for the current content of the obligation, which was questionable, by new rights and obligations. Thus, all rights (the entire content of the obligation relationship), or only some of them, can be settled between the parties. If all the rights are being replaced, only those rights are exempt that the party making the contract could not consider.

Settlement presumes replacement of current obligation by an obligation arising from settlement. Apparently, settlement is close to privity novation, but it may replace only a part of the current obligation content; then it will be close to cumulative novation.

Settlement agreement is not voidable in case of mistake about what is disputed or doubtful between the parties. Securing rights effected by the settlement continues but is limited by protection of third persons.

(c) Delay of Debtor (Mora Debitoris)

28. The Civil Code stipulates that a debt (obligation) must be fulfilled properly on time. If the debtor has not fulfilled his/her debt properly on time, he/she is in delay. Both performance terms must be given cumulatively to deem the obligation discharged by performance. So a debt fulfilled on time but having legally relevant flaws has the same effects as a debt not performed within the time stated.

Besides the general stipulation for debtor's delay in performance arising from an obligation, the Civil Code specifies special legal consequences for the particular types of obligations. We will deal with them in relation to the respective obligation types.

Debtor's delay causes a change in the obligation content, resulting either in a change of creditor's rights and debtor's duties or in the rise of new creditor's rights and new debtor's duties. These may be further classified as follows:

- Once the debtor is in delay and a minor breach of the contract is at issue, the creditor is entitled to determine an additional reasonable period of time for performance. If the debtor does not perform within this time either, the creditor is entitled to withdraw from the contract. If a major breach is at issue, providing an additional period of time is not required. If the performance is severable, the creditor may withdraw from the contract effective only in a part of the performance. Legal consequences of the withdrawal involve all types of contracts, that is, also the contracts registered by a State notary's office in the respective procedure. Thus, the debtor's delay does not affect his obligation to fulfil the debt before the creditor's withdrawal from the contract has become effective.
- The right to withdraw from the contract as mentioned in the previous paragraph does not involve the so-called fixed contract. In the case of an obligation where the time of performance was stated quite strictly and it is obvious beyond any doubt from the contract or from the nature of things that the creditor loses his economic interest upon delayed performance, under the Civil Code such a contract is cancelled *ex lege*. Only in the case where the creditor insists on the performance, he must announce it without an unnecessary delay to the debtor and thus the obligation continues to exist.
- In the case of a monetary claim, the creditor is entitled to demand interests for delay when the Civil Code or implementing provisions do not stipulate a duty to pay fees for delay for the particular case (the amount of interest and fees for delay are stated by the respective implementing provision).
- If the debtor is in delay with the performance, the risk of loss, damage or destruction of a thing has passed upon him, unless the damage would have occurred anyway.
- The debtor's delay entitles the creditor to claim compensation for the damage caused by the delay. In the case of monetary performance delay, the debtor will be liable only up to the amount, which is not covered by the interest for delay or by fees for delay.

(d) Creditor's Delay

29. Creditor's delay occurs when the creditor has not accepted any performance from the debtor, or when the creditor failed to provide the necessary cooperation to the debtor in performing the obligation.

Creditor's delay results are as follows:

- during the time of the creditor's delay the debtor's delay does not have legal consequences;
- if the thing was a performance, the risk of damage of the thing lies on the creditor for the time the creditor is in delay unless the damage is caused by the debtor;
- if costs or a damage incur to the debtor during the time of the creditor's delay, the creditor is bound to compensate;
- if the nature of the debtor's performance so allows, the debtor can fulfil the debt through an official deposit (section 1953, C.C.).

The provision on the option of withdrawal from the contract in the case of the debtor in delay applies to delay of the creditor too.

§2. FORMAL AND EVIDENCE REQUIREMENTS

I. Formal Requirements

30. Under the Czech law, contracts can be made, unless stipulated otherwise by law or agreed by the parties, in a form that does not give rise to doubts about the content of will as manifested by the parties to the contract.

Everyone has the right to choose any form of legal proceedings, unless restricted in agreement or by law – section 559 C.C. The forms of a juridical act may have various forms, the basic classification being written or oral ones. The Civil Code does not specify the oral form. The written form is further classified into a simple form (private register) and that of an official record (public register). The simple written form requires a written expression and a signature. The written form is maintained in legal proceedings made by electronic or other technical means to capture its contents and identification of the acting person. The text itself may be made by any technical means (unless expressly stipulated for some juridical acts that it must be made in one's own hand); the signature must be in one's own hand. Replacing signature by technical means is admissible only where it is ordinary (section 561, al. 2). If the juridical act has been carried out by electronic means, it may be signed electronically under section 40, al. 3 of the Act No. 227/2000 Col. Requirements of the written form are met if a juridical act has been carried out by electronic means enabling recording of the juridical act and denoting the person who has carried it out. In contracts, manifestations of the parties may be made in different documents; in real property conveyance only, the expressions of the parties must be included in the same document. In the cases stated by law, the written form is made more restrictive by the signature attestation as prescribed. The form of the official record is a qualified written form; at present, it is a public notary's record. Public charter is a document issued by a public authority within its jurisdiction or any instrument which declares a public register law; this does not apply if they have such defects that it looks as if it was not a public document. If a fact was confirmed in a public charter, it constitutes full proof of origin of document, of the time of the instrument, as well as of the facts confirmed in the public charter, until the contrary is proved.

Lack of the form required by law or by agreement of parties results in the contract being void; lack of the form as agreed on is related to the contract being voidable (sections 582, 586, 588 C.C.).

If the form of legal conduct has not been agreed upon by the parties, invalidity may be claimed only if performance has not been made yet. This also applies in the case of not keeping the form required in Part IV, C.C.

A. Tender

31. Tender is a specific manner of concluding a commercial contract, enabling selection of the most suitable offer from the bids. Therefore, tender is used mainly for contracts where one of the parties is a public authority and where the tender is obligatory, declared and conducted exactly according to the rules stipulated by a special law. In commercial obligation relationships, it is the case where a person (the announcer) on his/her own will announces the tender for the most suitable proposal to conclude a contract. The tender is not yet an offer for making contract, only a call to submit offers for its making. The call for tenders done in the form of a tender is related to legal consequences. In announcing tender, the terms of competition are required to be published.

B. Public Tender

32. Newly, it is possible to conclude a contract on the basis of a public tender. With a public tender, the offeror addresses unspecified persons with an offer to conclude a certain contract. The offer has to have elements required by law for an offer to conclude a contract. The contract is concluded with the person who first declares in conformity with the terms of the offer that he/she accepts the offer. The other offers must be revoked by the offeror. A public tender may be revoked before accepting the offer in the same manner in which the offer has been publicized.

C. Auction

33. Auction is a way of making a contract when the contract is concluded by knocking a hammer.

II. Contract under Seal

34. The 'obligation' contract under seal is not mandatory in the Czech contract law. *See* more in V. Function of Notary and Notarial Instruments.

III. 'Solemn' Contracts

35. Solemn contract as a manner of concluding contracts is unknown to Czech law. An exception is marriage solemnization, which, however, is not generally deemed a contract.

IV. Evidence Requirement

36. As for a special form of contracts required by law or agreed on by the parties, *see* the previous text.

Only in cases stated by law, some declarations of the parties to the contract require a special form of the so-called official record, which can either be a public notary record or in some cases also a record made by bailiffs under the Judgment Enforcement and Execution Act. (*See* more in V. Function of the Notary and Notarial Instruments.)

V. Function of the Notary and Notarial Instruments

37. Under the Czech law, the notary is a public clerk, his/her duties involving, among others, drawing up contracts in the cases where an official form of the notarial record is required by law or by agreement of the parties.

This form is required by law in the following instances:

- generally for all juridical acts of such persons who are unable to read or write, not even while using a technical device enabling them to get acquainted with the text of the document to be signed and to sign them in turn with their own hands;
- where it is specified by law (cf. forms of testament, establishing certain types of companies).

The position of the notary is regulated in the Notary Act. The notary is appointed for life by the Notary Chamber. The notary candidate must have a university degree in law and a preliminary practice. There are quantitative limits for establishment imposed by the Notary Act and by the decisions of Notary Chamber. The notary is obliged to comply with high professional standards and must exercise due care in the execution of his/her activities. The notaries are subject to disciplinary jurisdiction executed by the Notary Chamber.

The Notary Act furthermore includes provisions in the form of notarial records and other requirements that must be met. The notarial record has the value of an authentic act (public instrument).

The notary has the power to issue a special notarial act (e.g., a contract) with an execution clause that may serve as a writ to execution.

The task of the notary lies especially in the field of law of matrimonial property (contracts regulating property relationships of the spouses, etc.), law of artificial legal persons (establishing, modification, transfer and termination of companies, associations, foundations, etc.: since 2016, only notaries can establish, modify etc. the legal persons by way *online*), law of succession (e.g., testamentary dispositions) and law of immovable things.

VI. Burden of Proof

38. The distinction made between 'obligation of means' and 'obligation of results' as a general concept is unknown to Czech law.

Czech law distinguishes situations in which the expression of will and manifestation of will are not identical, that is, the cases when the content of will is different from what follows from its manifestation. As manifestation of will as a feature of a juridical act necessarily presumes compliance of will with its manifestation, in the case of inconsistency of will and its manifestation, an essential feature of the juridical act is missing. Various inconsistency variants of a will and its manifestation may occur, one of the basic criteria of their classification being the relationship of inconsistency and the awareness of the acting person. Thus deliberate and accidental inconsistency of will and its manifestation may be distinguished.

(a) *Deliberate inconsistency of will and its manifestation is one-sided where one party's will and its manifestation are inconsistent, and both parties are aware of it.*

One-sided deliberate inconsistency of will and its manifestation arises as a mental reservation or a one-sided simulation.

Mental reservation (inner reservation) means that the acting person includes a reservation in the will he/she manifests but does not explicitly manifests that reservation. Thus, the will and its manifestation of the acting person are not consistent to some extent; the acting person is aware of it but the other parties of the juridical act or third persons are not because the reservation is of inner nature, not being explicitly manifested.

One-sided simulation (pretending) of some will is of similar nature; the acting person manifests a different will from the one he/she really has. He/she realizes this fact, but he/she pretends to other party and third parties to have the will he/she has manifested.

The consequence of one-sided deliberate simulation results from the fact that the will manifested is not serious. Therefore, it results in the juridical act being non-existent sections 552, 554).

A shared deliberate inconsistency of will and manifestation occurs when, in bilateral or multilateral juridical acts, all parties manifest something different from what they really want. Their real wills are consistent, so are their manifestations, but there is no consistency between their real wills and real manifestations. It is a simulation in which the parties pretend to carry out a juridical act (relative simulation). A simulated (fictitious) juridical act suffers from inconsistency of will and its manifestation; moreover, the will manifested is not serious. Therefore, they are sanctioned by being held non-existent under the Civil Code (sections 552, 554). Also, in this case, voidness of the act may not be claimed against the party who considered it unveiled. A veiled juridical act is a dissimulated juridical act. If this veiled juridical act corresponds with the will of the parties and meets all the requirements, it is valid (section 555, al. 2).

(b) *Accidental (unknown) inconsistency of will and its manifestation is a mistaken manifestation.*

§3. Liability and Negotiations

I. Pre-contractual Liability

39. For the parties to be able to conclude a contract properly, several fundamental terms must be met, including:

(a) terms concerning the entity involved, that is, legal personality and capacity of a person to make the contract in question, or the capacity of the person representing the party in concluding the contract;
(b) the title of the party to the contract subject matter;
(c) when negotiating the conclusion of the contract the parties have to declare all circumstances for the conclusion of the contract;
(d) if a contractual party acts against the legitimate expectations of the other party he/she is liable to such a party for damage (section 1728 C.C.).

There are in the Czech Civil Code pre-contractual duties between a business and a consumer in the consumer contracts:

- Information duties (general duty to disclose information about goods and services, specific duties for the business delivering goods or services to consumers, duty to provide information when concluding contract with a consumer who is at a particular disadvantage, information duties in distance communication and information duties when concluding consumer contract by electronic means). Generally, the information must be clear and precise, and expressed in a plain and intelligible language.
- Duties to prevent input errors.
- Duty to negotiate in accordance with good faith and fair dealing (good morals).

II. Breakdown of Negotiations

40. Generally, the persons are free to negotiate and are not liable for failure to reach an agreement (section 1728 al. 2 C.C. unless they do not intend to conclude the contract).

A. *Termination*

41. Contractual negotiations may be terminated prior to conclusion of the contract, the basic principle being that the offeror or offeree are both bound by contractual manifestations. It is necessary to distinguish the possible terminating of the offer by the offeror and offeree (about this subject matter, *see* more in Chapter 1, section 1, I. Offer and Acceptance).

In Czech Civil Code, we can find the *clausula rebus sic stantibus* as an instrument of the deliberation of one of the contractual parties from the duty to conclude a future contract (section 1788 al. 2 C.C.).

The former Czech Law did not state the concept of *culpa in contrahendo* as the written norm, either. But at the beginning of the twenty-first century, the Czech Constitutional Court accepted the principle of legitimate expectation, subsequently applied by courts, that in the cases when a person refuses to make a contract without a sufficient reason and the other person suffers loss, then such a person is awarded damages. The new Civil Code includes *culpa in contrahendo* in sections 1728–1730).

Chapter 2. Conditions of Substantive Validity

42. Contracts arise upon two unilaterally addressed juridical acts. For their rise and for their validity, it is necessary that their addressing be mutual, identical in content and expressing assent to contract. For more about the right to revoke or reject the offer or acceptance *see* Chapter 1, section 1, I. Offer and Acceptance.

The contract content will be specified mainly by the offer; for some types of contract, the law prescribes which essential parts must be contained in the contract in question, otherwise it does not exist (cf. contract for sale and purchase as an agreement on the subject matter and the price). The contract may also contain the content of the contract on a future contract, the non-mandatory rules included in law, etc. The instant of concluding the contract is stipulated by sections 1725 and 1745, under which a contract is made upon the instant when acceptance of the offer becomes effective. Silence or inaction themselves do not imply acceptance.

The same principle also applies to carrying out multilateral juridical acts where expression of will of more than two parties is required and the substance of which is also assent, mutual will and harmonious will of all parties to the contract.

Sometimes another fact is required (e.g., assent of other parties or ruling of a relevant authority) to be added to the unilateral will manifestation, or manifestations of will of two or more parties. The offer may be accepted, though, by providing performance in conformity with the offer.

Formation and subsequent existence of a juridical act is one of the prerequisites for its validity.

Formation and validity must be distinguished from a juridical act when becoming effective, that is, from a situation when effects of a juridical act are connected with such a will manifestation by a rule of law. In the majority of cases, the rise, validity and effect of a juridical act fall within one instant. In specific cases, the law binds the effect of a valid juridical act to meet further requirements. Such process is regulated in the new Civil Code under section 1762, al. 1 and 2; for the cases where ruling of a respective authority is necessary for a contract, the contract takes effect only upon that ruling. Unless an application for the respective ruling has been filed within a one-year term following the conclusion of the contract, the contract is deemed to have been cancelled. The same applies if the offer was rejected.

§1. Essential Elements

43. For the contract as juridical acts to have capacity to give rise to proper legal consequences it is necessary – in addition to existence of its respective terms – to meet quality requirements, the fundamental elements or essentials of a juridical act. These essentials usually involve the following:

(a) capacity of the parties;
(b) will to contract;
(c) manifestation of will;
(d) will in relation to expression;
(e) subject matter.

(a) Capacity of the Parties

44. The prerequisites of the parties to carry out juridical acts are, first, their capacity to have rights and duties and, second, their capacity to act. General capacity of a natural person in juridical acts (capacity to act) is regulated by sections 30–37, of juridical person by sections 161–166 Civil Code. The effects of incapacity are contained in section 582 al. 1 Civil Code.

If a party lacks capacity to act, the juridical act becomes void. The law does not expressly stipulate this effect; however, it is implied in the nature of this essential condition. Such a case may occur with some juridical persons whose capacity is of a specific nature (extent).

The lack of capacity to perform juridical acts results in voidness of the respective juridical act. It will be so in the case of minors if they carried out a juridical act inconsistent with their limited capacity, in the case of persons incapacitated by a court ruling, or in the case of persons with limited capacity. A juridical act carried out by a person not incapacitated or restricted in capacity by a court ruling will also be void if such a juridical act was performed in a state of mental disorder that made the person incapable to act (section 581). This provision relates to cases of temporal mental disorder (including drunkenness) as well as the cases in which the court could have ruled on a restricted capacity but has not done so yet.

(b) As for the Will Essentials, Usually the following Ones are Mentioned: Existence, Freedom, Seriousness, Lack of Error

45. Existence of Will. The requirement of real will means inevitability of its existence. In this regard, including real will as an essential condition among the essentials of the juridical act is redundant because it overlaps with the necessity of will existence as a feature of a juridical act. If there is no will, no juridical act is formed. Therefore, such a juridical act must be deemed non-existing (*non negotium*) – section 551 C.C.

The cases where the will is missing are clear, but sometimes the will of an acting person appears to be present, even though it is not. An example is the will enforced by physical duress comprising physical pressure upon the party who expresses the will of the person exercising duress upon him/her instead of his/her own. This means that the will of the acting party does not exist here.

Freedom of Will

46. Free will is freedom to act, that is, freedom of a party to decide in what legal relations he/she will participate through juridical acts the basis of which being their will.

Free will does not exclude general limitations and conditions stated by law for juridical acts.

Under civil law theory, free will is deemed excluded when the following circumstances are present: physical duress, wrongful threat and distress.

By physical violence, another person forces the acting person to express the will of the person exercising violence upon him/her, instead of his/her own. It is of no significance if the violence comes from the other party or from the third party. Neither is decisive whether the other parties to a juridical act were aware of physical force exercised upon the party or not. For physical duress to be legally relevant, it must be illegal, and a causal relationship must be found between it and the expression made by the person under pressure; that is, the performed expression must be the result of duress. Because physical duress excludes the will of the acting person, the fundamental element of a juridical act is missing, and therefore, such an act is futile and as such void under the Civil Code.

Wrongful threat is an illegal threat affecting the will of a party causing in him/her a reasonable fear of injury that is threatened. In this manner, the will of the person under threat is created contrary to his/her real will. The difference between physical violence and wrongful threat is that in wrongful threat the person under threat expresses his/her will, but such a will that is deformed by a wrongful threat. While in the case of violence the acting person has the only option – that is, to express the will of the person exercising violence upon him/her – he/she has two options in the case of a wrongful threat: either not to subdue and to express his/her own real will or to subdue and express the deformed will. Avoidance of the contract entered due to the wrongful threat is possible also in the case where such wrongful threat was exercised by a third party, even if the other party of the contract was not aware of the third party's duress.

Wrongful threat is relevant under law while satisfying the following conditions:

- The threat must be wrongful, that is, the threat comprises something that is not allowed (e.g., to cause bodily harm) or the threat comprises something that the threatening person is entitled to use, but not for the purposes to make another person to perform a certain juridical act (e.g., by filing a complaint against somebody for an actually committed offence if the contract is not made).
- There must be a causal link between the threat and the expressed manifestation; the threat must incite fear influencing directly the will of the person under threat.
- The threat must be of such intensity as to be able to give somebody real fright.

The seriousness of the threat to cause fear is judged individually, considering both the subjective situations of the acting parties and the particular circumstances involved.[7]

Wrongful Threat Makes a Legal Act Voidable (§588 C.C.)

47. Free will is excluded also by usury (sections 1796–1797). Usury is defined by law as misusing distress, inexperience, mental weakness, anxiety or carelessness of the another party and gaining a promise of performance which is in a gross imbalance regarding the mutual performance. Usury is sanctioned by voidness.

7. See also Decision of Constitutional Court from 06.11.2007, II. ÚS 3/06

Seriousness of Will

48. The will of a party is not serious if the acting person does not want to give rise to legal consequences that are related with such a will and its manifestation under law. A broader interpretation of seriousness of will – when the will does not intend to invoke legal consequences – also includes mental reservation and simulation (*see* the explanation on accordance of will and manifestation).

Lack of serious will has to be assessed as an error leading to a futile legal act. Pursuant to the Civil Code, the lack of seriousness of will results in a non-existent legal act (section 552).

Lack of Error

49. An error – similarly to lack of serious will – presents discord between legal consequences that the party intended to give rise to and the consequences actually arising. The error of will means wrong or insufficient awareness of legal consequences arising from a juridical act (this differs from an error of expression which is a discord of will and expression). The consequences of legal invalidity relate only to a certain qualified error of will (such error is deemed legally significant). Other errors cause no such legal consequences. An error is of legal significance if:

- it is concealed (the party acting in error is not aware of it);
- the other party shared in its rise;
- he/she incited it intentionally;
- he/she incited it in another way or he/she must have known about it (in this case an error must be based on a fact that is decisive for the juridical act to be carried out, the so-called substantial error (mistake to content)).

Substantial error may concern the following circumstances:

- legal grounds (*error in negotio*) – the party incorrectly presumes that the will is directed to a certain act while it is another act in fact (the exchange of deed of donation instead of contract for sale);
- the subject of a juridical act, either its identity (*error in corpore*) – the party thinks to be buying the thing A, but subject of the purchase contract is subject B, or the properties of the subject (*error in qualitate*) – the party is buying for example, an antique that is not actually an antique;
- persons (*error in persona*) involving a change of the person;
- other circumstances without which a juridical act would not be carried out.

Error of will may result in voidability (by 1991, an option of withdrawal was stipulated).

(c) Essential Requirements for Manifestation Are Intelligibility, Definiteness, and in Some Specified Cases Also a Form

50. The expressing of will is unintelligible if its content is not clearly said, and it is not possible, according to an interpretation, to find out what have been in fact expressed.

Unintelligible manifestation of will cannot give rise to legal consequences, and therefore, it is considered non-existent (section 553). This does not apply if the manifestation of the will between the parties has not been sufficiently made clear.

Civil law is based on the principle of no-form expression, which means that a juridical act may be carried out in any form, unless specifically stipulated by law. Even if no formalities have been prescribed, the parties may agree to carry out a juridical act in a certain form. Therefore, formalities can be imposed by statute or by contract.

The forms of juridical acts may be various, the basic classification being written and oral ones. The oral form is not prescribed by the Civil Code. The written form is then classified as simple and by official record. The simple written form requires the act to be recorded in writing and a signature appended. Typically, the written form means that the content is given in a document. The text itself may be made by any technical means (unless stipulated that they must be made in one's own hand). The signature should be in one's own hand. If replaced by technical means, it is admissible only where it is ordinary. If a juridical act is performed by electronic means, it may be signed electronically. The written form is made permanent if a juridical act is carried out by electronic or other technical means, enabling recording the content of the juridical act and denoting the person who carried it out which requires attachment of an authorized electronic signature according to the court practice. The written form in the cases as specified may be made stricter by a prescribed certified signature. The form of the official record is a qualified written form; at present, it is a public notary's record. The following forms are required by law:

- in general for all juridical acts of those who cannot write or read, not even while using special equipment enabling them to get acquainted with the content of the documents signed, and to sign it with their own hands;
- in specially stipulated cases (cf. form of last will establishing a capital company).

Lack of the formalities prescribed by law results in voidness, while lack of the agreed formalities results in voidability.

Voidness due to lack of form is related to special situations, not occurring in other reasons for voidness. Under section 2997 paragraph 1 Civil Code, accepted performance, based on a juridical act that is void as a result of lack of form (both under law and under contract), is not deemed unjustified enrichment. It cannot be said that it is a validation of a void legal act because by the stipulation quoted earlier, only one of the possible consequences of a void legal act is excluded – namely, the duty to return unjustified enrichment obtained from a void legal act.

(d) The Essentials of the Relation of Will and Its Manifestation, and Their Conformity

51. Civil law analyses in detail the situations where the will and its manifestation are in discord, that is, the cases when the content of will is something different from what follows its manifestation. The will manifestation as a feature of a juridical act necessarily presumes a concord of the will with its manifestation; in the case of discord of the will and its manifestation, a fundamental feature of a juridical act is missing. Various combinations of will and manifestation discord may occur; one of the essential criteria of their classification is the relation of discord and the awareness of the party. Accordingly, known and unknown discords of will and manifestation are recognized.

A known discord of will and manifestation is one-sided: when the will is in discord with the manifestation of one party, or common (bilateral or multilateral) when the will and the manifestation are in discord on all sides, and both parties know about it.

One-sided known discord of will and its manifestation comes as mental reservation or one-sided simulation.

Mental reservation means that the party makes a reservation in the will he/she manifests without explicitly expressing that reservation. It means that the will and manifestation of the acting person are in discord to a certain extent; the acting person is aware of it, but the other parties to the juridical act or third parties are not because the reservation is of an inner character, it is not explicitly manifested.

One-sided simulation (pretending) of will is of a similar character; the party manifests something different from his/her true will; he/she is aware of the situation but pretends before other parties to have the will he/she is manifesting.

The consequence of one-sided intentional simulation follows from the fact that the will expressed is not serious. Therefore, the result is non-existence of the juridical act (section 552 Civil Code).

A common (shared) known discord of will and manifestation is given when in a bilateral or a multilateral juridical act all parties express something different than they want in fact. Their real wills are in accord, so are their manifestations, but there is no concord between their real will and the manifestations expressed. It is a simulation when the parties pretend to carry out a juridical act even though they want to carry out none (absolute simulation) or when they pretend to carry out a certain juridical act to disguise another juridical act (relative simulation – *dissimulation*). Simulated juridical act suffers from discord of will and manifestation; moreover, the will manifested is not serious. Civil Code therefore sanctions it by non-existence of legal conduct. If by a legal conduct another legal conduct is supposed to be concealed then it will be judged according to the actual will (section 555, al. 2).

Unknown discord of will and manifestation is an error of manifestation. Also, here one-sided and two-sided discords may be recognized.

Unilateral unknown discord arises when the acting person's will is in discord with its manifestation in a unilateral juridical act or the will and its manifestation of one party in multilateral juridical act. These are the situations in which the actor expresses that he/she wants something but in fact wants something else without realizing error in his/her manifestation (slip of a tongue – *lapsus linguae*, mistake in writing, etc.).

Similarly as errors of will, various types of errors in manifestation are recognized:

- error in a juridical act – the acting person has expressed a will for a juridical act to be carried out, even though he/she in fact intended to carry out another act (e.g., instead of the intended donation he/she expressed the will to make a contract of purchase);

- error in the content of a juridical act – the error in the effects to be brought about by the juridical act – for example, error in time, place and manner of performance;
- error in subject may have various forms, for example, error in identity of the thing, error in kind (quality), property and amount of a thing;
- error in the person of the contracting party, for example, erroneous person gifted under a deed of donation.

If manifestations of will of two or more parties are in discord, the consent to contract is missing, and thus a juridical act in theory may not arise. This is true if the discord concerns a substantial matter, but discord does not prevent a juridical act to arise if it is only formal and may be resolved by an interpretation. The non-substantial elements of a juridical act affected by discord will be governed by the relevant stipulations.

Two-sided discord gives rise to voidability, too.

(e) Subject Matter Must Be Possible and Allowed

52. The possibility of subject matter in a juridical act should be understood as the possible conduct of the party in correspondence to rights and obligations arising from the juridical act. Most often, it will be performance. Possibility of performance arising from a juridical act is objectively an inevitable requirement of validity of a juridical act. If the subject matter of a juridical act is performance that cannot be provided, such act cannot be legally binding (voidness).

The possibility of subject matter of a juridical act must not be made identical with the existence of a thing. It is not the thing that is impossible but the performance related to such a thing, for example, donation of such a thing is impossible, etc. When the subject matter of performance is a generic thing, the performance is actually impossible in practice, too. However, there can be an exception – namely, with the things that ceased to be produced or imported and are no more available in the period from the moment of making the offer and the actual contract making (e.g., in mail-order sale and purchase).

Impossibility of the subject matter of a juridical act results in its voidness (section 580 al. 2, section 588 C.C.), but the impossibility must be absolute (physical). This also concerns the cases when performance is so extraordinarily difficult that, with regard to good morals, the owing party cannot be rightfully expected or demanded to overcome the obstacles. Any other level of impossibility of performance cannot be deemed an impossible performance. Also, such performance is not impossible that is only relatively impossible, that is, such that is impossible only due to subjective reasons (i.e., only in the view of the owing party).

Impossibility must be initial; that is, it must exist upon the rise of the juridical act. If such impossibility arises only after the juridical act occurred, it results in termination of the existing obligation.

An allowed juridical act means that such act is legally possible; that is, it is judged according to rules of law. A disallowed subject matter results in the juridical act being void. Examples include the subject matter being inconsistent with law, evading law or being contrary to good morals:

- Inconsistency with law is evident mainly when certain behaviour is expressly prohibited by law. Inconsistency with law may concern the content, too, which is not expressly worded but is implied in the stipulation.
- The subject matter of a juridical act evades law if it does not violate directly the requirement given by law but is clearly against good manners and public policy (section 588, C.C.). Such an act will be declared void by the court even without a motion.

In the sphere of civil law, the principle 'everything is allowed what is not banned' is applied.

Chapter 3. The Content of a Contract

§1. General Explanation

53. The content of a contract means legal consequences of forming, changing, or terminating a legal relationship, or rights and obligations. The content of a legal relationship is thus stated (even though indirectly) as forming, changing, or terminating upon a juridical act.

The content of a contract is determined by the parties within their autonomy of will, but it must respect certain cogent stipulations of legal rules, either stipulating content essentials or excluding elements in some juridical acts. The contract content may also be influenced by the decision of a respective authority as well as by the content of non-mandatory rules unless their effects were not excluded by the acting person's conduct.

Contract terms are classified according to their frequency and their legal relevance into substantial, regular and incidental as follows:

- Substantial terms are such that are unconditionally required. These terms are given by legal norms (e.g., subject matter and price in contract for sale) and can be specified by the parties; that is, they are of subjective nature (enabling the parties to denote such element essential which they themselves consider important).
- Regular terms are such that occur as a rule, but their absence has no effect on the rise and validity (e.g., agreement on the time and place of performance).
- Incidental (subsidiary) terms are such that arise only incidentally and irregularly.

These are mainly conditions, time determinations and some others.

Conditions are such subsidiary provisions by which the consequences of the juridical acts are made dependent on unknown circumstances (conditional juridical acts). Such an uncertain circumstance may be a future fact that is not known to the parties – whether it will occur or not or a fact that will certainly occur but the parties do not know when – or a past fact about which the parties do not know that it had already occurred. C.C. (section 548) distinguishes condition precedent and condition subsequent; when in doubt the condition is considered to be the subsequent one.

Time fixing as a provision in a juridical act is similar to subsidiary condition. It means that effects are conditioned on the expiry of time. Unlike a condition, in the case of time fixing, it is certain that the time stated will expire, and the effects of the juridical act will come into existence or terminate. Time fixing may be of two types: in the first case, the effects of a juridical act will come into existence only after a certain time; in the other case, the effect of a juridical act will terminate after the expiry of the fixed time (time-limited rights and obligations are discussed in more detail later).

I. Consequences

54. Consequences of a contract may be the rise, the change or the termination of a juridical act (rights and obligations). These consequences concern persons affected by the juridical act and things that denote legal relations (rights and obligations) established, changed or terminated by the contract.

As a rule, the contract has effects only for the parties who made it. This conclusion arises also from the character of civil law regulation method, where the party in a civil law relationship may not one-sidedly interfere with legal relations of other individuals, except for the cases given by law. The exception is a contract in favour of a third party (*pactum in favorem tertiis*). It is a contract in which one party (the debtor) promises the other (the creditor) to perform in favour of a third party (sections 1767–1769). Such a case is an insurance contract for insuring property, life or health of third parties. Another exception is a contract for performance of a third person which, however, does not directly bind the third person by its effects (section 1769).

As for the subject matter, the contract has consequences only for the legal relationship directly involved. An exception is accessory relations linked in their existence with prime legal relationships (as a rule, security relations on securing a claim).

II. Grounds and Consequences of Invalidity

55. Such consequences are linked to the contract inconsistent with rules of law and can be divided as follows:

(a) Putative juridical act (Nullity of the juridical act).
(b) Invalidity.
(c) Withdrawal from an invalid act.
(d) Contesting.
(e) Liability for invalidity of juridical acts.

(a) Putative juridical act (Nullity of the juridical act)

56. A juridical act is deemed putative (*non negotium*) if it lacks one of the substantial features. This mistake occurs if the will is lacking in the contract or if the content of the contract is uncertain or not understandable (sections 551–553). A seeming legal conduct is not taken into consideration (section 554).

(b) Invalidity

57. Invalidity in relation to a juridical act or a legal relationship means that the juridical act or the relationship is void or has been avoided. There are two types of invalidity: voidability and voidness.

The voidability as included under the Civil Code is typical of the new Czech private law. Legal conduct is needed to be considered rather voidable than void.

Voidness

58. Void juridical acts are deemed existing but invalid if certain requirements or essentials sanctioned under law by voidness are missing. No legal consequences arise from such juridical acts for the parties or third parties. It is characteristic that voidness arises directly under law (*ex lege*) without the necessity to claim the consequences by either party. Voidness may be claimed by anyone legally involved, not just by the parties. The court will consider voidness ex officio. The grounds for voidness include inconsistency with law, a sharp inconsistence with good morals, a clear breach of public policy or conduct not allowed from the very beginning.

The effects of voidness of a juridical act can be considered according to time and subject matter.

Because for the time, voidness is effective as a rule *ex tunc*, the juridical act is void since its origin. The voidness is effective immediately. Voidness persists even though the grounds of such voidness became extinct later; a void juridical act may not become valid later. Voidness cannot be rectified through confirmation of an obligation. Only the so-called conversion is possible, which means that if a void juridical act complies with the essentials of another juridical act, it may have consequences of that juridical act (section 575).

As for the extent, the effects of voidness are considered according to whether the whole act, or only its part, is void. The solution is found in section 576, under which only that part of an act that is affected by the grounds for voidness is void. The part of the act not affected remains valid being a separate whole.

Voidability

59. The essence of voidability is the fact that a juridical act, which is deemed valid, induces legal consequences as if valid by the time its invalidity has been claimed or declared by the respective authority. Voidability is taken into consideration only upon the objection brought by the entitled party. Pursuant to the Civil Code, it is the person affected by such an act – that is, the party to a juridical act or a third party who was affected by the ground of voidability. A person who has caused invalidity may not object the voidability of juridical act.

The question of the qualified claiming of the effects of voidability is not quite satisfactorily resolved in the legal theory. There is an opinion that the principle of equality of the parties must be respected; therefore, it is possible to induce consequences of voidability in two ways:

(1) The part affected by voidability will claim voidability in relation to the other party by a unilateral juridical act who will accept the objection, and they both together take measures for removing negative consequences of the voidable juridical act.

(2) If the other party will not accept the objection, the party wishing consequences of voidability to occur must file a complaint with the court for invalidity to be declared. In such cases, legal consequences of voidability will occur only on the grounds of the court decision.

However, a different opinion has been accepted by the majority of legal writers (which also prevails in court practice and is supported by the authors of this text) based on distinguishing direct and indirect voidability. In direct voidability, claiming voidability by the party entitled is sufficient. For the effects of voidability to arise, an out-of-court notice is sufficient by which the entitled party claims voidability (it is a real one-sided addressed juridical act). The voidability becomes effective the instant the notification reaches the other party or all the parties to the act.

In the case of indirect voidability, the voidability of a juridical act must be declared by court. The Civil Code establishes direct relative voidability (section 568).

The possibility to claim voidability is bound to a certain time limit. The court practice, however, holds that this right of the party is subject to the prescription of a three-year period starting to run from the moment when the entitled person learns the reasons of voidability. The period of limitation expires in ten years at the latest. This time limit begins to run on the day of carrying out the juridical act.

The grounds of voidability of juridical act are, in comparison with grounds of voidness, less serious; therefore, personal incentive of the party affected is expected to avoid the consequences of the invalid act. This also includes lack of the agreed formalities for the expression of the juridical act, error, deception, threat of violence, lack of consent of another party, etc. (sections 580–587).

Voidability affects juridical acts in respect of time and subject matter, too. As for the time, voidability as a rule is effective since the beginning (*ex tunc*), but unlike voidness, only on the condition that the respective claim for voidability has been made. Unlike voidness, in the case of voidability a validation may be admissible. If the flaw that might have led to voidability was removed or rectified, invalidity cannot be claimed.

(c) Withdrawal from an Invalid Act

60. Withdrawal is a unilaterally addressed juridical act of the entitled party intended to prevent the effect of the act. An invalid act is deemed existing and valid and thus causing legal consequences; however, one can withdraw from it. The option to withdraw from an invalid act is available exclusively to the entitled party; that is, the party affected by the invalidity with which the option to withdraw is linked.

The effects of withdrawal become effective at the moment when the expression of withdrawal has reached the other party, while effective *ex tunc*, that is, retroactively since the time when the juridical act was carried out, unless prescribed by law or agreed by the parties otherwise. The effects of invalidity of a juridical act by which the entitled party withdraws from an invalid act occur automatically (per se) and are not dependent upon the decision of the other party or the court. The court may only check whether the juridical act by which the entitled party withdraws meets the given terms or not. The effects of withdrawal are definitive; validation or a following confirmation of the act is not possible. The effects of withdrawal might be removed only by carrying out a new juridical act.

As for the extent, withdrawal has the effect identical to invalidity.

The grounds of withdrawal due to invalidity of the juridical act are not generally regulated by the Civil Code. A special regulation of withdrawal from the contract is included in rules of consumer law; in that case, it is not exclusively a consequence of a mistake of the contract (cf. sections 1818, 1829–1837, 1846–1850, 1861–1865). Withdrawal is admissible also in other cases not resulting from invalidity of a juridical act.

(d) Contesting

61. Contesting of juridical acts means an option to claim legal consequences ineffective only towards a certain person (creditor). (*See* more later in Chapter 4, section 4 *Actio Pauliana*)

(e) Liability for Invalidity of Juridical Acts

62. Liability consequences connected with invalidity of a juridical act originate as a consequence of invalidity or withdrawal from an invalid juridical act. The following liabilities are possible:

- mutual restitution duty, that is, the duty of parties to return everything they have received due to the invalid juridical act; general provisions on unjustified enrichment will be applied, but it should be noted that performance under the juridical act that is invalid due to lack of formalities agreed by the parties is not deemed unjustified enrichment;
- duty to compensate damage arising as a result of an invalid juridical act. A special provision is included in section 587; the person who has caused a legal conduct by threat or deception shall always provide compensation for the injury arisen from that.

Influence of the Time on the Legal Relationships

63. Legal relations as well as rights and liabilities may be formed for a period of indefinite duration and as such are unlimited in time, or their duration is limited for a fixed time. There are rights the existence of which is not limited in time (property right, personal rights, personality rights) and for which no time of limitation applies. However, there are rights that are, by their nature and designation, limited for a certain time. These include the right to use a borrowed thing, right to temporary dwelling, etc. A third group is made by the rights that may be restricted for a certain time, but this restriction does not arise from their substance and designation (e.g., restriction of lien for a certain period).

The extinction occurs by the lapse itself on the last day of the time stated, and no further legal facts are necessary.

Preclusion

64. The consequence of preclusion is the extinction of a right that is not exercised in the preclusive period of time. Therefore, two conditions have to be met in order for the right to extinguish:

(1) lapse of a certain period (precisely given by law);
(2) failure to exercise the right within this period.

If both conditions have been fulfilled, the following legal consequences of preclusion occur:

- a subjective right extinguishes (along with the claim);
- the respective authority takes into consideration the preclusion ex officio;
- if performance is carried out after the preclusion period lapsed, it is deemed an unjustified enrichment as its legal grounds have become extinct as the result of preclusion (*see* explanation of unjustified enrichment).

Preclusion terms are rather exceptional in civil law and must be explicitly stated by law – namely, in such a manner that, upon failure to exercise the right in this period, the right becomes extinct. These are mostly time limits for claiming liability for damage – deadlines for complaints. Preclusion terms cannot be prolonged, and their running is not suspended or interrupted. There are exceptions to this general rule when a certain time is not included in the preclusion period.

Prescription (Statutory Limitation of Right)

65. Unlike the previous consequences of preclusion, a right under prescription does not terminate by lapse of time but it is considerably weakened, because the debtor is released from the duty to perform. A right extinguishes unless exercised within the period stated by the Civil Code. By the lapse of time, the first phase of a right extinguishing is fulfilled if two facts have taken place: the lapse of *tim*e and the failure to exercise the right.

When the period of prescription expires, the legal relationship between the owing party and the entitled party continues; a subjective right or a claim does not become extinct, only the claim becomes conditioned, that is, dependent on whether the owing party claims the lapse or not. Upon the lapse of time, the right to claim that lapse has arisen to the owing party, if the entitled party demands the performance of his/her subjective right. The entitled party may claim protection of his/her right with a respective authority even after the lapse of the statutory time, because his/her right has not become extinct (unlike in preclusion). The owing party may also voluntarily carry out his/her obligation even after the lapse of period of limitation, and it will not be deemed as an unjustified enrichment of the entitled party as legal grounds for performance have not become extinct.

The second phase of prescription comes at the moment when the entitled party has claimed his/her right in court. Then it is necessary to distinguish the instances in which the owing party has not exercised his/her right to claim the lapse of time and in which he/she has claimed it. If the owing party has not claimed prescription, the respective authority does not take it into consideration ex officio. Claiming the prescription in relation to the facts from the first phase of lapse causes the right to terminate; the right becomes unenforceable, and the respective authority cannot impose it. The subjective right continues to exist, though; it is only considerably weakened (as a result of the claim extinction), existing in the form of a natural obligation. If the performance occurred in this second phase, again it would not be unjustified enrichment.

Not all rights are subject to prescription. With respect to their nature and function, the prescription is not applied to personality rights, personal rights and personal property rights. Under the law, limitation does not apply to:

- ownership rights, right to division of a common thing, right to having a necessary road built and right to buying out an easement;
- lien if there is a debt surety;
- right to maintenance but not to individual partial performance;
- rights from deposits in banks and current accounts if the deposit relationship continues.

Deadlines and Time Limits

66. For the consequences of right extinction, a time prescription is required. The Civil Code stipulates the time prescription in such a manner that it lays down the rules for determining its beginning, length and specification of some obstacles influencing its running.

The beginning of the period of prescription is determined either objectively or subjectively. In general, the beginning is the day when the right could have been exercised for the first time (*actio nata*). Such a day is the one when the right could have been claimed in court for the first time. Pursuant to the new C.C. (section 619), the right may be exercised for the first time when the entitled party has learned, could have learned and should have learned about the circumstances determining the commencement of the limitation period. Other rules for the commencement of limitation period are set forth in sections 620–627 for rights to damages, to surrendering unjust enrichment, to compensation of an injury of a minor who does not have full legal capacity, to partial performance, to getting financial means from a financial institution after termination of a contractual obligation, and rights arising from damage to a transported thing, and, in general, rights to insurance performance. This period is generally set forth for three years.

In addition to the above-mentioned three-year limitation period, the law also recognizes another one. The beginning and length of the period of limitation is specified in some cases:

- property right is statute-barred in ten years at the latest since the day of its maturation unless provided otherwise by law;

- the parties may negotiate a shorter or longer limitation period, the shortest one being, however, one year and the longest one fifteen years;
- a right recorded in the public list is statute-barred in ten years since the day when it could have been exercised for the first time;
- a right to performance from life insurance is statute-barred in ten years;
- right to performance from liability insurance is statute-barred at the latest when the right to damage compensation or injury not covered by the insurance is statute-barred;
- right to damages is always statute-barred in ten years at the latest and damage caused intentionally in fifteen years since the day when the damage or injury occurred;
- right to surrendering unjust enrichment is statute-barred in ten years at the latest and, if caused intentionally, in fifteen years since the day when the unjust enrichment occurred;
- for the rights of an entitled heir to demand the inheritance to be released, the period of prescription does not terminate until six months since the court decision about terminating the probate proceeding becomes effective;
- right awarded by a decision of a body or recognized by the debtor;
- other special periods of time, their beginning and their running are regulated in sections 629–653 C.C.

These are especially the following situations:

When dealing with time, it is suitable to deal with the so-called combined times that are those in which several times of prescription (with an objectively or subjectively stated beginning) are applied concurrently in law. In these combinations, various situations may occur; a right extinguishes upon the lapse of a subjectively stated prescription but no later than on the lapse of an objectively stated limitation. The following instances may objectively occur:

- The beginning of the subjective term occurs during an objective term and, by its lapse, the whole subjective term lapses. A right extinguishes upon the lapse of the subjective term.
- The beginning of the subjective term occurs during the objective term but, by its lapse, only a part of subjective term has lapsed, and another part has lapsed only after its end. The right will extinguish upon the end of the objective term as it is evident from the wording 'a right extinguishes no later than'.
- The beginning of the subjective terms occurs only after the objective term has lapsed. The right extinguishes upon the lapse of the objective term, and the subjective term is entirely irrelevant.

The running of the period of prescription is continual since the beginning to the end unless an obstacle occurs with which the law connects the consequences stated. A change in the person of the creditor or the debtor has no influence on the run of the period of limitation. The new debtor may also claim the prescription against the new creditor.

Based on the existence of relevant obstacles, the following effects may occur:

The period of prescription has not started if a fact occurred from which the period of prescription starts to run as usual but, due to an obstacle predicted by law, the beginning is postponed. Pursuant to the Civil Code, the following situations are included:

- in the case of rights of persons who must have a statutory representation and do not have it, or in the case of rights against these persons;
- in the case of rights between statutory representatives and minors, and other represented persons; this does not apply if interests and repeated performance are in question. The same applies to rights between spouses.

If the beginning of the period of prescription has begun and the time runs but during its course an event occurrence that causes putting off the end of the period of prescription that would otherwise occur, we can consider the period of prescription not coming to an end. The following cases are included:

- If during the period of limitation such an obstacle occurred, then the course of the period of prescription has been interrupted. The parts of the period of prescription that expired before and after the obstacle will be added up. The Civil Code establishes the following cases for period of prescription interruption.
- If the creditor during the period of prescription brings a suit to court or another respective authority to satisfy the claim and duly continues in the proceeding.
- If the right was duly granted and enforcement of judgment was proposed to court or another respective authority.

The cases mentioned here are sometimes designated as an interruption in a narrower sense, and the cases stated earlier when the period of prescription does not begin or end are designated as an interruption in running in a broader sense.

If such an event occurs that causes suspension of the period of prescription in running, it means that the part of the lapsed period of prescription is not taken into account (becoming legally irrelevant), and the period of prescription starts to run from the beginning again. Pursuant to the Civil Code, the lapse of the period of prescription occurs:

- if the right was granted by an effective court decision or another authority;
- if the right was acknowledged by the debtor in writing as for the grounds and the amount.

In both cases, a ten-year period of limitation is applied.

§2. Interpretation

67. A juridical act is interpreted whenever applied and whenever it is necessary. The purpose of the interpretation is to establish the will of the acting person expressed in the content of the juridical act. The interpretation then ascertains the existence of real consequences of a juridical act, that is, formation, changes, or termination of legal relationships, or rights and obligations.

Usually the content of a juridical act is ascertained from the verbal form of the juridical act. This, however, does not always provide an unambiguous path to ascertain the real content of will manifestation; therefore, other circumstances in which the will manifestation was presented must be also taken into consideration. The content cannot be derived merely from the name of a juridical act.

An interpretation of a juridical act is done by the acting persons themselves (mainly in exercising the rights arising from it) or by the respective State authorities (especially the courts that decide about the exercised rights).

For interpretation of juridical acts and legal provisions, the different legal rules are generally applied. An interpretation of rules of civil law is included in Chapter I C.C.; an interpretation of types of legal conduct in sections 555–558 C.C.

In interpretations of juridical acts, special attention should be paid to unification of results of all manners and methods of interpretation. Particular aspects of the content interpretation of a single juridical act and all respective aspects in their mutual links should be understood within this framework.

Legal acts are considered according to their content. If the real nature is hidden under another type of legal conduct, this real nature is decisive. Acts expressed in words or otherwise should be interpreted consistently with the will of the person who carried out the respective juridical act. If the acting person's intention cannot be found out, the usual expression is attributed to it. In interpretation what will be taken into consideration is the practice between parties, the context of acts and also expressed intentions of the parties. When in doubt about the meaning of the used expression, the interpretation is made to the detriment of the person who used the expression as the first one. When negotiating with an entrepreneur (P2B) and in negotiations between entrepreneurs (B2B), the usual meaning of the expression between the parties, or business customs, has an increased importance for the interpretation of legal acts (section 558, C.C.).

§3. Conditional Contracts

68. The contractual terms regulating a right or obligation may provide that it is provided upon the occurrence of an event of which the parties do not know that it may occur at all; or an event that certainly will occur, but the parties do not know when; or a past event that the parties are unaware of.

The condition may involve an objective fact (e.g., reaching an age) or a subjective fact (concluding a contract).

The purpose of the condition enables the party to carry out a juridical act also at the time when not all facts are known that will be involved when the juridical act will be carried out. This applies in the instance when both the rise and the termination of legal consequences are tied to the fulfilment of the condition.

Conditions must be objectively possible and allowed. A condition must be objectively possible, that is, there must be a possibility to carry it out. Physical objective impossibility of a suspensive condition results in invalidity of a juridical act in respect of annulling the condition (invalidity of the condition as a whole or partially); objective impossibility of resolutive condition results in invalidity of the condition (the condition is disregarded).

Condition is admissible if it is not contrary to law, is consistent with good morals or with public policy. An inadmissible condition should result in invalidity of the juridical act or a condition.

In the Czech law, conditions are classified according to various criteria, one of the most significant being dependence of the juridical act effectiveness upon the fulfilment of a condition. Therefore, conditions are divided into suspensive and resolutive. Suspensive conditions are linked with effectiveness of a juridical act in such a manner that the juridical act made dependent on such a condition takes effect upon the fulfilment of the condition, at the time when the juridical act exists as valid but is not effective. After fulfilment of the suspensive condition, the juridical act becomes effective as a rule because the condition has been fulfilled. The juridical act does not take effect if fulfilment of the condition was intentionally caused by the party obtaining benefit from it, even though he/she was not supposed to cause it. In such a case, fulfilment of the condition is regarded as not executed. The ultimate impossibility to fulfil the condition results in the final decision that the juridical act will not take effect in the future, either, and the same consequences occur due to prevention of the condition fulfilment, that is, rendering fulfilment impossible through some kind of interference. If the fulfilment of the condition was intentionally prevented by the party gaining benefit from that, the condition is considered fulfilled (section 549).

Resolutive conditions take effect in such a manner that, by fulfilling them, the effect (relevant right or obligation) of a juridical act comes to an end. This means that the juridical act was effective, but upon fulfilment of a resolutive condition, the effectiveness expires. Before the condition was resolved, a state of uncertainty had existed based on the question of whether the juridical act may become ineffective or not. By fulfilling the resolutive condition, the effect of a juridical act expired, as a rule upon the instant of its fulfilment with the effect *ex nunc*. A juridical act does not become ineffective if the fulfilment of the condition was caused intentionally by the party who benefited from it, but the party was not supposed to cause it. Finally, the decision that the condition cannot be fulfilled results in the juridical act to continue and ceases to be conditional. Preventing the fulfilment of a resolutive condition has the same effect; in the case when the fulfilment of the condition was prevented intentionally by the party benefiting from it, the juridical act then becomes unconditional.

Another criterion for the conditions classification is the nature of conditions. Therefore, we distinguish positive conditions (depending on whether a certain situation will occur, has occurred or exists) and a negative condition (depending on whether certain situation will not occur, has not occurred or does not exist).

From the viewpoint of the party influencing a condition to occur, we may distinguish the conditions that can be fulfilled (potestative), accidental (causal) conditions and mixed conditions. Potestative conditions are those the content of which is a fact that can be performed by the party. It means that their fulfilment or failure to fulfil can be influenced by human will. Fulfilment of accidental conditions is out of human will. Thus, fulfilling these conditions depends on circumstances that are not under the control of persons.

Chapter 4. Privity of Contract

§1. The Rule of Privity of Contract

69. The Czech law of contract is based on privity of the contract. This means that:

(1) either party may not one-sidedly impose his/her will on the other party;
(2) either party may not one-sidedly decide in his/her own dispute (*nemo est index in propria causa*).

I. Third Parties and the Contract

70. The rules mentioned earlier means that a third party is not bound by agreements of contract parties, the exceptions being the cases established by law or the cases when the third party actively joins the contractual relationship concluded between/among other parties.

II. Contract for the Benefit of a Third Party

71. An initial requirement of equality of parties prevents third parties from being affected by contractual agreement. However, the Czech law of contract admits that to conclude a contract for the benefit of a third party, the effects of such contract are bound to the consent of third party.

Obligations for the benefit of a third party arise upon a contract by which the debtor (*prominent*) is obliged to the creditor (*provisor*) to perform upon the contract relation to the third party (*tertius*). The tertius will not participate actively in this contract relation. The tertius becomes a creditor, being entitled to demand performance, in dependence on the content, nature and purpose of the contract; usually at the moment when he/she has manifested his/her will in a legally relevant form to accept the performance (the form of will manifestation is not prescribed; it may only be implied). The debtor also retains all objections he/she might have against the creditor. The creditor himself/herself may claim performance, unless agreed otherwise. If the tertius refuses to accept the performance, the promisor is entitled to demand performance – but only if so agreed in advance. If the tertius refuses his/her consent to the performance arising from the contract, the promisor is entitled to demand the performance, unless agreed otherwise (section 1768).

Any contract may be concluded for the benefit of a third party unless it is inconsistent with its nature; that is, it is inconsistent with law, is inconsistent with good morals or with public policy. Typically, such contracts are included in the Civil Code as, for example, insuring third parties, or vouchers, etc.

Obligations for the benefit (but also to the debt) of third parties must always be distinguished from agency. For these obligations, a third person is a party to the contract whereas the agent is not.

III. Contract to the Debit of a Third Party

72. The new Civil Code recognizes obligations to the debit of third parties although they represent a principal violation of civil regulation of equality of parties due to the fact that one party obliges the other that is not a party to the contract for the benefit of the creditor. For this reason, the concept of obligations to the debit of third parties is not acceptable in this pure form. Contractual obligation cannot arise for a person who himself/herself is not a party to the contract. Therefore, parties to the contract may only agree on the so-called promise of intercession of the debtor with a third party to provide performance. Then it is the breach of promise of intercession of the debtor with the third party that will be deemed as a breach of obligation, not failure to perform by the third party for the benefit of the creditor. However, if a person undertakes that tertius will perform something for the creditor, in the case of default such a person is obliged to compensate the creditor for the damage (section 1769).

§2. Transfer of Contractual Rights and/or Obligations

73. It is socially desirable to enable one or more elements of the structure of contract relations to undergo certain changes while they endure. In some cases, a change may be deemed so principal that the changed obligation is required by law to be deemed a new obligation. In other cases, the current obligation, upon undergoing changes, has retained characteristic features of the original obligation to such an extent that it is not considered as a new contract but merely as an altered contract.

Changes in contracts may arise only if, during the existence of the original obligation, certain legal situation arises that is prescribed by law as a change of certain terms only. The alteration of contract may be performed under an agreement of the parties or a unilateral juridical act, an official ruling, or an illegal conduct of a person (delay). Legal grounds for a change of an obligation are the original legal situation along with a new situation causing the obligation to change.

Contract relations are usually classified according to which contract element is involved in the change. These changes are classified as:

– changes involving the parties;
– changes in the content and subject matter of an obligation.

Changes in the content and subject matter of an obligation are included in one category because a change in the subject matter causes, in turn, a change in single rights and obligations of the parties. (For more about changes in the content, *see* Chapter 1, section 1, IV. Modification of Contract.) The Czech law recognizes the following kinds of changes involving the parties:

(a) assignment of a claim (*cessio*);
(b) assumption of debt – substitution of a new debtor;
(c) accession to an obligation – adhesion to liability for debt;

(d) transfer of contract (contractual position).

(a) Assignment of a Claim

74. The term and the rise of the legal relationship. Assignment of a claim is an alteration of obligation wherein, based on a certain legal situation (most frequently a contract between a debtor and a creditor), a new creditor (also called a cessionary or assignee) replaces the previous creditor (also called assignor) in the relationship while the original relationship continues to exist.

As for this type of change regulated under Czech law, we distinguish an assignment of a claim established by the agreement of the parties (*cessio voluntaria*) and an assignment of a claim independent of the will of the parties (*cessio necessaria*, forced assignment of claim), which can be either a statutory assignment of a claim (*cessio ex lege*) arising directly from rules of law or an assignment of a claim arising from a court decision (*cessio judicaria*). While statutory assignment of a claim is stipulated for particular situations in various legal provisions (e.g., providing performance to the creditor by the guarantor under the surety on behalf of the debtor) and the same applies to the change of the creditor based on a court decision (a number of such instances are stipulated under the rules of Civil Procedure, e.g., enforcement of judgment by ordering a claim), general provisions of contract law under the Civil Code concern contractual assignment of the rights.

Voluntary assignment of the rights arises from a written contract based on which the previous creditor, the assignor, transfers his/her claim upon a new creditor, the cessionary. The written form of the agreement is not necessary.

The debtor is excluded from the procedure because, under law, his/her consent to the transfer of the claim is deemed unnecessary for the claim transfer to be valid because the debtor's situation undergoes no change by the claim transfer. Regarding the obligatory nature of the claim transferred, the Civil Code stipulates instances in which a claim cannot be transferred. Such claims are excluded due to their nature, which becomes extinct no later than upon the creditor's death (e.g., the right to recover compensation for injuries and for a difficult social position and assertion), claims the content of which would change upon the change of the creditor (e.g., an obligation to teach music), and claims not enabling legal recourse through enforcement. Besides, the possibility of an assignment of a claim may be excluded in advance by an agreement of the creditor and the debtor (section 1881).

Content of Legal Relationship. The content of an assignment of a claim, that is, mutual rights and obligations between the parties, will differ according to whether the claim has been ceded for money or gratuitously. In the case of an assignment of a claim subject to payment, the assignor is liable to the cessionary up to the amount of the received payment with the interest for the duration of the claim at the time of the cessation.

The assignor is liable for the claim, existence and recoverability only up to the amount of the claim obtained along with ancillary rights. The assignor's liability, as stated earlier, is absent, if the assignee has not claimed the debt ceded in court without an unnecessary delay and in other cases mentioned in section 1885 C.C. In other cases, the rights and duties among the assignor and the cessionary are regulated adequately by the provisions of the C.C. on fulfilling a debt (sections 1914–1925).

Contrary to that, if the claim has been ceded gratuitously, the assignor, as may be deduced from the arguments given in the provisions mentioned earlier, has no such liability.

At the instant of the assignment of claim, the assignor forfeits the claim and the right to performance, which is obtained by the cessionary. The condition is that the debtor must be notified about the assignment of the claim; that is, the duty to notify rests on the assignor. However, it is also possible for the cessionary to notify but in a satisfactory manner (e.g., by submitting the written text of the contract). Before the debtor has been notified about the claim ceded, he/she may perform for the benefit of the assignor or to settle the claim otherwise with him/her. The assignor is bound to hand over to the cessionary and transfer upon him/her all legal remedies and security tools concerning the ceded claim and to give him/her all the necessary information.

The necessity to protect creditor's rights has led to the provision that, even after the assignment of a claim, the debtor keeps all defences (remedies) he/she had against the initial creditor at the time of the assignment of the claim. Moreover, the debtor may claim his/her objections against the assignor and also against the cessionary, even though they have not yet matured at the time of the assignment of the claim.

If the ceded claim has been secured by a surety, the assignor is bound to notify the person who provided the surety about the assignment of the claim or the cessionary is bound to prove the assignment of the claim.

Even if a claim has been effectively ceded, the assignor may, when the cessionary agrees and does not seek the claim himself/herself, claim the debt from the debtor in his/her own name and at the cessionary's cost.

A special type of assignment of a claim is assignment of a set of claims. This is possible if the set of claims is sufficiently identified, e.g., by the time or by an identical legal reason (section 1887 C.C.).

(b) Assumption of Debt: Substitution of New Debtor

75. *The term and the origin.* An assumption of a debt arises when a new debtor joins the existing obligation relationship instead of the current debtor.

An assumption of a debt arises in cases presuming it upon an agreement between the debtor and the third party with the creditor's consent. A mandatory written form is not required by law.

The consent may be given to both the new and the original debtors.

Even though the content of obligation basically does not change by the debt assumption, the surety provided by the third party is preserved only if this person has expressed his/her consent to the debt assumption (section 1890 C.C.).

The content of legal relationship. Because there is a valid assumption of the debt, the new debtor is bound to perform instead of the original debtor, and the creditor is entitled to claim the performance from him/her. The content of obligation has not changed upon the debt assumption; thus, the new debtor has all defences available as the original debtor had to assert them against the creditor, except the manifestation directed to set off the claim of the original debtor towards the creditor. There are no mutual claims of the creditor and the new debtor; thus, setting-off is implicitly excluded, because the original debtor has withdrawn from the debt.

If a contract of a debt (obligation) assumption has been made between debtors but the creditor either did not consent to or refused his/her consent to the debt assumption, such a contract is effective under law only in relation to the original debtor and the new debtor, but it does not have legal effects for the creditor, who is entitled to demand performance from the original debtor and to refuse accepting performance from another party. Therefore, the new debtor would have to give, under such a contract, performance to the original debtor, who will in turn give this performance to the creditor. Such a duty is also owed by the person who pledges himself/herself to the debtor to ensure performance for the his/her creditor (section 1889 C.C.).

(c) Accession to an Obligation: Adhesion to Liability for Debt

76. The term and the origin of the legal relationship. Accession to debt is a type of a change of the contractual relationship that takes place when a third party joins the current creditor and obliges himself/herself to perform his/her obligation on his/her behalf. In this case, adhesion to the obligation is effective without an agreement with the creditor. A mandatory written form is not required by law.

The content of legal relationship. Following an effective accession to a debt obligation, the creditor may demand performance both from the original and from the new debtor, or from both. Among the parties of accession to debt arises a relation of passive solidarity. This, however, applies only to the relationship of co-debtors towards the creditor.

Under law, no recourse relationship arises between the debtors after one of them has duly performed. It could be taken into consideration only if solidarity relationship was agreed between co-debtors in advance. By performing the debt by one of the debtors, the obligation of the other to perform becomes extinct, too. Unless the original debtor wishes to be bound by the new debtor as a result of the debt performing (based on inner relationship between the co-debtors), he/she should precede the cessionary in performing.

77. A situation similar to accession to a debt arises as a result of taking possession of property (sections 1893–1894 C.C.). If someone takes possession of all property from the alienor, or a proportionally specified part of it, he/she becomes jointly with the alienor the debtor from the debts which are connected with the acquired property and which he/she has known or must have known about.

(d) Transfer of Contractual Position

78. Transfer of the whole contractual position of a party to a third person is known in Czech Law as a specific (named) type of transfer of rights and obligations (sections 1895–1900 C.C.). If it is not excluded by the nature of the contract, the contractual party may assign a third person his/her rights and duties from the contract or from a part of it. Such a procedure may occur: (a) if the assigned party agrees and (b) there has been no performance of the contract yet. Neither this type of contract is required by law to be in writing.

The assignment of a contract is effective against the assigned party since his/her consent; if the party has consented in advance then it is effective since notification of the assignment made by the assignor or since proving of the assignment of the contract by the cessionary. The consent of the assigned party may include reservations against the assignor. By the assigned contract coming into effect, the assignor releases himself/herself from his/her duties to the extent of the assignment; this may be prevented by the assigned party using the procedure pursuant to section 1899 and all his/her objections against the contract remain preserved.

§3. The Special Case of a Subcontract, for Example, the (Nominated) Subcontractor in Building Contracts

79. Czech contract law does not specify a subcontract. However, the terms 'subcontract' and 'subcontractor' are used, especially in building contracts. These contracts are not expressly stipulated by law and thus it is up to the parties' will to define its content. Nevertheless, the law regulates particular situations in subcontracts. For example, section 2589 provides an option for the contractor to have the work done by a subcontractor; section 2630 provides a joint responsibility of the contractor and the subcontractor for defects, etc. A special regulation of subcontracts can be found in public law regulations concerning public procurement.

§4. *Actio Pauliana*

80. The Roman *actio pauliana* is applied under the Czech Civil Code to the institute of relative ineffectiveness of the juridical act (cf. sections 589–599).

Actio pauliana is based on the option to claim ineffectiveness (invalidity) of legal consequences towards a particular person only. The creditor may demand the court to determine that the debtor's juridical acts, if they reduce creditor's recoverable claims, are ineffective. It is possible to raise objections against juridical acts performed by the debtor. Ineffectiveness of payments made by the debtor may be sought by the creditor under conditions and within periods of time set forth in section 590. Ineffectiveness of non-payment actions of the debtor may generally be sought against the debtor's contractor, against the person who benefited from the debtor's actions, against his/her heir or against the person who has acquired the assets as a successor of a legal entity during its transformation. Against another legal successor of the debtor, it is possible to seek ineffectiveness in cases specified in section 594 al. 2.

On the basis of ineffectivity, it is also possible to get satisfaction from the property which was taken away from the debtor's assets in this manner (section 595).

Chapter 5. Termination of a Contract

81. The particular manners of termination of an obligation can be classified according to various criteria.

With regard to whether – upon termination of an obligation – creditor's claim has been discharged, we distinguish obligations as:

(a) obligations with the creditor satisfied (*cum satisfactione creditoris*), which are, for example, performance, novation or settlement;
(b) obligations without the creditor satisfied (*sine satisfactione creditoris*), which are, for example, withdrawal from the contract, impossibility or waiver of a right.

Under the Czech law, termination of a contract can be made in the following ways:

- §1. Debt Fulfilment: Performance and Breach. Voucher. Alternate performance.
- §2. Impossibility and Hardship: Unforeseen Impossibility.
- §3. Withdrawal from the Contract.
- §4. Setting-Off (Unilateral and By Agreement).
- §5. Agreement on cancellation Obligation (Novation).
- §6. Waiver of a Right.
- §7. Remission of a Debt.
- §8. Discharge.
- §9. Lapse of Time.
- §10. Death of the Debtor or the Creditor.
- §11. Preclusion of Rights.
- §12. Debtors Delay under 'Fixed' Contract (Debtor's delay – *mora debitoris* and creditor's delay *mora creditoris*: *see* IV. Modification of the Contract).
- §13. Merger of Debts.

§1. Debt Fulfilment: Performance and Breach

82. Performance is a juridical act by which the debtor (or a third party, the surety, etc.) gives performance to the creditor who accepts this performance (it is not a bilateral juridical act). Mutual consent of the parties is not necessary – this is basically given in a juridical act itself, giving rise to the obligation, and in law governing rules for performing an obligation. For example, a debtor can perform even without the creditor's cooperation by placing a thing in an official deposit (section 1953 C.C.), and this act will be deemed as performance, although the respective creditor's act will be missing in this case.

The essentials of performance of a contractual obligation are:

(a) existence of an obligation;
(b) unilateral act of the debtor, directed to provide performance;

(c) unilateral act of the creditor, who accepts the performance.

Parties to performance are, as a rule, identical to the parties to the obligation.

On the debtor side, it is mostly the debtor himself/herself; this is explicitly stated by law for the obligations. The subject matter is performance that must be provided by the debtor in person, because performance by a third person would be of a different quality. Performance, however, may also be provided by a third person, who is bound to perform under law, by an official ruling, or under a contract. Thus, the surety will be bound to provide performance if the debtor has not performed his/her debt upon the call of the creditor (e.g., a salary payer who has not complied with the contract of payroll deduction; a spouse performing on behalf of the other spouse, if it is the case of community property of spouses; performance provided by an agent; etc.). Recourse between the party who performed instead of the debtor and the debtor is possible only if stipulated by law. Performance provided by the third person should be based on specific legal grounds. If there are no grounds, such performance establishes the relationship of unjustified enrichment and a duty of the benefiting person to return the performance. The law provides an option for the debtor not to perform personally in sections 1935–1938 and then in the case of voucher (*see* hereinafter). The debtor who performs through a third person is liable in the same manner as if he/she performed himself/herself. The creditor must accept the performance offered, with consent of the debtor, by a third person unless the performance is tied to the person of the debtor. By fulfilling the debt, the third person enters into the debtor's rights and the claim, including related rights, is transferred to him/her.

On the creditor's side, principally it is the creditor who is entitled to accept performance (the duty to provide performance to the creditor in person is stipulated under law), but it may also be a person different from the creditor.

Such cases occur most frequently if:

(a) the creditor must have a statutory representative due to his/her incapability to carry out the particular juridical act (taking over performance), and the debtor is bound to perform into the hands of the statutory representative in order to discharge his/her duty;
(b) the creditor will authorize an attorney to take over the performance;
(c) in assignment of claim by the time the debtor has been duly informed about the assignment of claim;
(d) the debtor performs for the person who will present the creditor's voucher on debt receipt, presuming that the debtor acts bona fide. In this case, the debtor can refuse to perform for the person who submitted the creditor's voucher of receipt only if it is a person different from the creditor.

Subject matter of performance can be determined either individually, or just by generic signs, stating that one of the parties (the debtor, unless stated otherwise) will make the selection of the particular things for performance (concentration).

In some cases, unity of performance is required. However, in certain cases performance in part (partial performance) is allowed by law:

- On principle, the debtor is bound to perform the obligation all at once. However, the creditor is not bound to accept a partial performance, either, only if so expressly agreed; if nothing is agreed in this sense, the debtor must pay the debt all at once only if it were contrary to the nature of the debt or to the purpose of the contract.
- For the rest of the cases, the debtor may provide also a partial performance, and the creditor is bound to accept it.
- Performance by instalments may be provided by the debtor, if so agreed with the creditor. The agreement presumes the deadlines agreed in advance and the amount of the instalments.

If the debtor is supposed to perform several debts for the same creditor and the performance is insufficient to cover them all, it is up to the will of the debtor to denote the debt for which the performance is intended as appropriate; if he/she fails to do so, the performance is appropriate for the debt: (a) that has already been demanded, (b) that is the least secured, (c) when the debts are secured in the same manner and that which is the first one to fall due. In the case of monetary obligation, the performance is to be appropriate first for: (a) specified costs, subsequently for, (b) interests on default, (c) interests, (d) principal if the debtor does not provide otherwise.

The subject of performance must be identical with the subject matter of the obligation. The creditor is not bound, with some exceptions (e.g., *alternativa facultas*), to accept another performance; such performance is not deemed duly provided and results in the debtor's delay. Another exception to be mentioned is a possibility to conclude a contract during the time of performance, under which the debtor provides a different performance from that originally stated, and the creditor accepts it. This institute, called traditionally *datio in solutum* – that is, giving instead of performance – is not expressly stipulated by the Civil Code and could be established by an atypical contract. Different is the case of *datio solutionis causa* – that is, giving for the purpose of performance. Here, the debtor transfers a certain thing or a right upon the creditor to satisfy the creditor not through the thing or the right itself (its usable value as a rule) but through its realization (e.g., through sale of the thing and obtaining the sale price, that is, realizing its economic value). Under this contract, the debt has been discharged upon the moment of value realization of the substitute performance.

The time of performance is stipulated by Civil Code only in general. Under the Civil Code, the following principles can be enumerated for determining time of performance:

- Determination of time of performance is principally left up to the parties.
- It is possible under law to leave the time of performance to be fixed by the debtor. If the debtor will not determine the time of performance, the creditor may, at any time, ask the court to determine it in consistence with circumstances of the case.
- In the cases of an increased interest in timely and accurate performance, time of performance is regulated by law.
- If time of performance has not been agreed on, regulated by law, or determined by court ruling, the creditor is entitled to demanding performance immediately

and the debtor is obliged to fulfil the debt without unnecessary delay after he/she was so required by the creditor. *See* more in sections 1958–1967 C.C.

In the case of incompliance with time of performance, the debtor (or the creditor, in respect to cooperation in performing) is in default, the legal consequences of which have been described previously.

Place of performance is defined as follows: a debt must be performed at the place determined by the parties' agreement otherwise in a place determined by law. The place of non-monetary performance will be the residence of the debtor. The place of monetary performance will be the residence of the creditor. In performing a monetary debt by mail or through a provider of financial services, the debt is to be paid up at the instant of adding the amount onto the account of the creditor's provider of financial services. If the debtor fulfils his/her monetary debt using a postal money order the debt is fulfilled by adding the due amount onto the account of the creditor's provider of financial services, or by paying the amount in cash to the creditor.

An agreement to perform through a third person is named Voucher (Assignatio) and Instrument – Voucher for Performance in Securities.

The holder of voucher is entitled to obtain performance from a third party (remittent) who is authorized to perform for the voucher holder on account of the remitter. A voucher is a compound obligation relationship under law that, even if classified among changed obligations, is aimed to perform through a third party.

A voucher is composed of three basic relationships, arising among three different parties. The parties are the creditor (assignee), the debtor (assignor) and a third party performing for the assignor. The respective relationships arising within a voucher are:

- Relationship of value, expressing as a rule the basic value of the relationship as a whole, which is the value of performance between the creditor and the debtor. This relationship arises through conclusion of an agreement between the assignor and the assignee, under which the assignor's debt will be performed by accepting performance from the third party.
- Relationship of remittance (payment) arises by authorizing the third party by the assignor to perform to the assignee. Two variants are possible here: if the third party is bound to the assignor to accept the voucher (e.g., based on a contract of current account or of credit already made), he/she is bound to accept the voucher. If there is no such relationship, an agreement on accepting the voucher must be made between the assignor and the third party.
- Relationship of payment arises by accepting the voucher by the third party and notifying the assignee about accepting the voucher. By this act, the assignee obtains a direct right to performance provided by the third party.

Voucher is a general type of obligation change and has no prescribed form in none of the juridical acts in which it arises and is executed.

As for the nature of performance voucher is an obligation with vicarious performance.

Because it is a three-party relationship, causing the risk of imbalance in legal relationships of the parties, these relationships are regulated by law in such a manner as to allow conditions for its balance.

Voucher may be cancelled only until it has been accepted by the third party.

A special form of a voucher regarding a security warrant is provided by the Civil Code. These are abstract obligations in which the cause need not be stated. If the warrant bears the claimant's name, it can be transferred by endorsement by which all rights arising from the warrant are transferred to the entitled person based on the endorsement.

The person who has accepted a voucher issued by a financial institution is bound to perform for the person for whose benefit the voucher was issued or transferred.[8]

I. Consequences of Performance

83. Performance results in discharge of the obligation. Other legal consequences are extinction of surety relations as an ancillary relation and the rise of the duty of the creditor to release to the debtor a receipt of debt fulfilment. If the performance was provided by a surety, a mutual recourse relationship arises between the surety and the debtor. Finally, as an expression of a functional synallagma, the right to demand performance from the other party arises for the party that has fulfilled its debt in mutual claims.

II. Breach of Contract

84. Obligations must be performed properly and on time. If one of these conditions has not been met, a situation called 'delay' occurs under Czech law. (Consequences of delay as a breach of contract are described in Chapter 1 IV. Modification of the Contract).

The remedies for breach of contract are not regulated synoptically in the text of Civil Code. One can summarize following remedies:

8. More detailed provisions describe regulations of bills of exchange and cheques.

In case of non-performance, the creditor is entitled: to withdraw from contract,[9] to demand default interest,[10] contractual penalty (if agreed), compensation of damage arose from non-performance.[11] The right to demand the original performance[12] is not in Czech civil law expressly regulated by the Civil code, but in practice considered to be a „natural" creditor´s right.[13]

In case of invalid performance, the creditor is obliged to notify and specify the failures. The remedies are different, when the failure is reparable or irreparable. If a defect can be removed, an acquirer may demand either a repair or supplementing what is missing, or a reasonable price reduction. If a defect cannot be removed and prevents the proper use of the subject, the acquirer may either withdraw from the contract or demand a reasonable price reduction.[14]

Alternate performance is possible if the creditor is unknown or absent, if the creditor refused to accept the performance without a reason, and if it is not certain who the creditor is, or for other significant reasons on the part of the creditor. In such a case, the debtor is entitled to depositing the performance with the court at the expenses of the creditor.

§2. Impossibility and Hardship: Unforeseen Impossibility

85. Obligation terminates when performance becomes impossible. Impossibility of performance is an objectively assessed impossibility, that is, not an impossibility based merely on the debtor's belief in impossibility to provide performance as required. Economic impossibility (hardship) does not fall within this category. Economic impossibility (hardship) is given if:

- an obligation can be fulfilled only in more difficult conditions or the cost of performance has increased;
- obligation can be fulfilled only with the help of another person;
- obligation can be fulfilled only after a specified period of time.

---

9. If, by its default, a party fundamentally breaches its contractual duty, the other party may withdraw from the contract if it notifies the party in default accordingly without undue delay after learning of the default (section 1977 Civil Code). If a default of one of the parties constitutes a non-fundamental breach of its contractual duty, the other party may withdraw from the contract after the defaulting party fails to fulfil its duty even within a reasonable additional time limit expressly or implicitly provided by the other party (section 1978 Civil Code).
10. A creditor who has properly fulfilled his contractual and statutory duties may require that a debtor who is in default of payments of a pecuniary debt pay default interest, unless the debtor is not liable for the default. The rate of default interest is determined by a government decree; if the parties do not stipulate the amount of default interest, the rate thus determined is considered to be the one stipulated (section 1970 Civil Code).
11. More marg.no. 85
12. Contrary to the international relations or to common law, where this right is limited or considered to be an extraordinary legal instrument.
13. The term 'specific performance' is not known in the Czech civil law. More for example: Jurčová, M. Právo na splnenie a možnosti jeho obmedzenia. (The right to the performance and the ways of its limitation). In: Právník, 2017, No. 2, p. 114 – 133, 175
14. Section 1923 Civil Code

It arises from the nature of things that performance may become impossible on the basis of merely individual assessment. Generic performance can be, if of extinction or destruction, or non-attainability, replaced by another performance and if it does not cause obligation extinction. In case of partial impossibility, the respective part of obligation terminates. However, contractual relationship terminates as a whole, if from the nature of contract or the purpose of performance (which was known to the parties at the time of the rise of the obligation) derives that the remaining part of obligation has lost economic value for the creditor, unless the creditor has informed the debtor without a delay that he/she insists on the rest of the performance being provided.

The debtor is obliged to notify the creditor without unnecessary delay about the impossibility of performance; otherwise, he/she is obliged to compensate the creditor for the damage incurred by that.

If, after concluding a contract, circumstances change to the extent that the performance arising from the contract becomes more onerous for one of the parties, it does not affect the party's duty to discharge the debt. This does not apply in cases provided under sections 1765 and 1766.

But if there is such a substantial change in circumstances that it creates a gross disproportion in the rights and duties of the parties by disadvantaging one of them either by disproportionately increasing the cost of the performance or disproportionately reducing the value of the subject of performance, the affected party has the right to claim the renegotiation of the contract with the other party if it is proved that it could neither have expected nor affected the change, and that the change occurred only after the conclusion of the contract or the party became aware thereof only after the conclusion of the contract. Asserting this right does not entitle the affected party to suspend the performance.

The affected party shall not acquire the right as stated above, if it assumed the risk of a change in circumstances.

Upon failure to reach agreement within a reasonable time limit, a court may, on the application of any of them, decide to change the contractual obligation by restoring the balance of rights and duties of the parties, or to extinguish it as of the date and under the conditions specified in the decision. The court is not bound by the applications of the parties.

A court shall dismiss an application to change an obligation if the affected party fails to assert the right to renew contract negotiations within a reasonable time after it must have ascertained the change in circumstances; this time limit is presumed to be two months.

§3. Withdrawal from the Contract

86. Under Czech law, it is possible to avoid an obligation by withdrawal from the contract.

In some situations, it is not possible to insist justifiably on strict adherence to the contract (*pacta sunt servanda*). An important interest of those involved in civil relations led to adopting some exceptions to the principle as stated earlier. One of the exceptions is the option to withdraw from the contract under Civil Code. The creditor is entitled to withdraw from a contract under general provisions on obligations under the Civil Code if it is agreed by the parties or if it is provided by law. A general legal option to withdraw from a contract is provided for the case of a substantial breach of the contract by a party. The breach is substantial if it is a duty about which a party knew or must have known before concluding the contract that the other party would not have concluded the contract if knowing that; other breaches of contract are not substantial. Other options enabling withdrawal are stipulated for specific obligation relationships stated under the Civil Code, especially in consumer relationships (*see* hereinafter).

Upon withdrawal, the rights and duties arising from the obligation terminate *ex tunc* (from the very beginning), which means that:

- the debtor is no more bound to pay;
- parties are bound to return one another the performance already provided;
- in principle, it is possible to withdraw from a contract if a part has not been fulfilled yet but if a partial performance is not significant for the creditor it is possible to withdraw from the contract completely;
- withdrawal does not concern the right to liquidated damages or to an interest on default if it has already become mature, the right to damages for breach of a contractual duty nor a covenant on withdrawal; withdrawal does not concern the securing of the debt; rights of third persons gained in good faith are not affected by withdrawal.[15]

§4. Setting-Off (Unilateral and by the Agreement)

87. Unilateral settlement is a unilateral juridical act by which a party sets off its mutual debt against the creditor's claim. The setting-off may be realized as soon as a party becomes entitled to demanding his/her claim and to paying his/her own debt. The obligations are discharged at the moment the mutual claims have become fit for setting-off. Claims fit for setting-off are those that may be brought before the court. On the contrary, uncertain or indefinite claims are not fit for setting-off. The conditions of one-sided set-off are as follows:

> It must be a type of debt for which setting-off is admissible. The setting-off of claims involving compensation for bodily or mental harm is excluded unless both debts are of the same kind. The same applies to claim of maintenance for a minor who is not fully competent.
>
> Setting-off by an agreement arises upon a creditor-debtor agreement, by which the parties set off their mutual debts in accordance with the conditions set by law. Setting-off by an agreement has the same legal ground as unilateral setting-off with the exceptions as follows:

15. See Decision of the Supreme Court from 26.06.2007, 32 Odo 622/2006

Setting-off by an agreement presumes mutual consent of the parties, also mutual debts, excluded from unilateral setting-off may be set off by an agreement. Only claims involving maintenance paid to minor children are excluded from setting-off by an agreement.

§5. Agreement on Cancelling an Obligation

88. The civil law generally knows an agreement on a new obligation (*novation*). This manner of obligation discharge is also called a novation of privity that is distinguished from cumulative novation, in which the original obligation does not become extinct, persisting along with the new obligation. Therefore, cumulative novation is usually listed among the ways of changing contractual relationships. As a modification of privity novation, the provisions of the new Civil Code regulating the termination of the obligation stipulate only the possibility to cancel the original obligation between the parties without replacing it with a new obligation (section 1981 C.C.). In this way also, a part of existing obligation may be cancelled.

§6. Waiver of a Right

89. Waiver of right arises by an agreement of the debtor and creditor, on the basis of which the creditor waives his/her right to demand the whole debt or its part to the debtor. Unlike debt remission, which is of a similar nature, waiver of right is typical for obligations involving non-monetary performance.

Waiver of rights is not expressly mentioned in the new Civil Code any more. Such an agreement is possible as a contract governed similarly by provisions on remission of debt (*see* the next section).

§7. Remission of Debt

90. Remission of debt is a manner similar to termination of an obligation by waiver of a right.

Remission of debt arises upon an agreement of both parties under which the creditor remits the debtor's debt. The debtor's consent is presumed unless he/she has declared without an unnecessary delay his/her disagreement, either expressly or by fulfilling his/her debt (section 1995 C.C.).

If the debt of one of the joint debtors is excused, or if it is excused by one of the joint creditors, it affects the others to the extent of their respective shares.

If the creditor excuses a duty of the person securing a debt, this does not affect the secured debt.

§8. Renunciation

91. Renunciation is typical of the existing obligations. The obligations may be renunciated if agreed by the parties or if provided by law.

Renunciation is a unilateral legal act addressed to the other party of the obligation.

The renunciated obligation terminates by expiration of the period of notice. An obligation renunciable without a period of notice terminates by the effectiveness of the notice, that is, by the notice being served on the other party.

The law provides special rules for contracts obliging someone to a continuous or repeated activity, obliging someone for the whole lifetime or for the period longer than ten years, or when circumstances have changed (sections 1999–2000).

§9. By Lapse of Time

92. A number of rights and obligations arising from obligation relationships become extinct by lapse of time for which they have been limited. An example may be lapse of the lease period. By lapse of time as an objective legal situation, either a single right or an obligation, or the entire obligation relationship, becomes extinct. Lapse of time as a fact giving ground for termination of rights, duties or the entire obligation may be fixed by law or by an agreement of the parties.

§10. Death of the Debtor or the Creditor

93. One principle of obligation law is permanence of the obligation in spite of various circumstances influencing either side. Therefore, for the sake of legal certainty, the Civil Code (section 2009) stipulates that a debtor's or a creditor's death does not principally result in the obligation termination, and by the death of either of them, the rights and obligations are passed to their respective legal successors. The exception is an obligation termination as a result of the death of the debtor, the content of which was a performance to be provided by the debtor in person. This is not exclusively a performance that cannot be provided by another person; the duty to provide performance by the debtor will derive from the content or nature of the obligation relationship. As for creditor's death, the Civil Code stipulates an exception, under which such debts that are restricted to the creditor's person exclusively are not passed on to the heir (e.g., claim to recovery for injuries and difficult social position and assertion).

§11. Preclusion of Rights

94. Unlike other ways of termination of obligation, preclusion is established mainly by lapse of time. The termination of rights and duties arising from an obligation is bound upon the cumulative existence of the two prerequisites as follows:

(1) lapse of time;
(2) inaction of the entitled party.

The termination of a right is taken into consideration by the court even if the debtor does not protest (section 654, C.C.).

§12. Debtor's Delay under 'Fixed' Contract

95. It may be concluded that termination of contract *ex lege* occurs as a result of cumulative coexistence of two facts:

(1) a debtor's delay in a fixed contract, that is, if the contract has stipulated a strict period for performance, and it arises from the contract or from the nature of the thing that the creditor has no interest in delayed performance;
(2) creditor's failure to notify without delay that he/she insists on performance in spite of the debtor's delay.

The effects of the termination of an obligation are the same as in the case of withdrawal from the contract. *See* section 1980 C.C.

§13. Merger of Debts

96. Merger as a reason for termination of obligation may arise due to various legal grounds; therefore, this type is listed separately as a type of termination under sections 1993–1994 of the Civil Code.

A merger of debts arises when the attributes of deport sand creditor are united in the same (natural or legal) person in the same capacity.

Part II. Specific Contracts

97. In explaining the particular contract types and their regulation under the Civil Code, attention is paid to the most important characteristic features of these contracts and to the most distinct feature distinguishing the particular contract from general provisions.

The following text is observed in explaining the particular types of contracts:

- the notion, legal regulation, creation;
- rights and obligations of the parties;
- liability;
- discharge.

If any of these essentials is missing, general provisions apply.

The Czech regulation of consumer contracts is explained in Chapter 1 in relation to how they are regulated in the Czech Code Civil.

Chapter 1. Consumer Contract: General Provisions

98. According to the EU legislation, consumer contracts involve no specific type of contract. Consumer contracts are contracts in which the consumer is in the position of a non-entrepreneur. Civil Code requires a supplier (the businessman) and a consumer, who are simply and explicitly defined for this purpose, to be the parties to the contract. A *supplier* is a person (natural person or a company) acting within its business or other entrepreneurial activity. A *consumer* is a natural person who, in making and performing the contract, does not act within its business or other entrepreneurial activity.

Consumer contracts under a specific regulation are:

- distance contracts;
- contracts concluded outside usual business premises;
- timesharing which is expressly designated by law as a type of consumer contract and regulated in sections 1852–1867 C.C.

§1. General Rules for Consumer Contracts

99. General provisions for consumer contracts are contained in sections 1810–1819 C.C.

Contractual agreements involving consumer contracts may not divert from the letter of law to the detriment of the consumer. Consumer protection requires cogency of legal rules; where the regulatory cogency is one-sided, more favourable terms may undoubtedly be bargained in favour of the consumer. A consumer may not waive his/her rights as granted by law, or otherwise weaken his/her contractual position.

The objective of this norm is to bar consumer contracts from containing a stipulation inconsistent with a bona fide requirement and avoid a significant imbalance of rights and obligations of the parties to the detriment of the consumer. This general clause is specified in the list of unfair terms.

Balanced positions of parties to the contract cannot be understood rigidly. There may exist spheres in legal relations between a consumer and a supplier where it is impossible to demand balance of terms.

The Civil Code contains the following list of unfair terms:

- excluding or restricting the supplier's liability for act or omission through which consumer's death or bodily harm was caused;
- excluding or restricting the consumer's rights to lay a claim in case of liability for defective product or damage caused;
- stipulating that the contract is binding for the consumer while supplier's performance is linked to a term satisfied exclusively upon the supplier's will;
- allowing the supplier not to release the performance provided by him/her to the consumer even if the consumer has not concluded a contract with the supplier or has withdrawn from the contract;

– authorizing the supplier only, and not the consumer, to withdraw from the contract without any contractual or legal ground;
– authorizing the supplier to repudiate, without reasons worth of special attention, the contract made for the time of indefinite duration without an appropriate notice time;
– binding the consumer to comply with the terms he/she could not have known about before conclusion of the contract;
– allowing the supplier to alter one-sidedly the contractual terms for reasons not stipulated in the contract;
– stipulating that the price of goods or service will be determined at the time of performance, or allowing the supplier to raise the price of goods or services without the consumer being entitled to withdraw from the contract, if the price agreed upon at the time of conclusion of the contract was considerably higher than that at the time of performance;
– ordering the consumer to perform all obligations even if the supplier has not fulfilled his/her own obligations as accrued;
– allowing the supplier to transfer the contractual rights and obligations without the consumer's consent, if recoverability of debts or the security of the consumer's claim security has been impaired as a result of the transfer.

The sanction for breach of the general clause or specified provisions is their voidness (*see* above).

The Civil Code states an interpretation rule under which, in case of doubts, the interpretation of a contract is more favourable for the consumer.

I. Distance Contracts and Contracts Negotiated Outside Business Premises

100. The new *C.C. includes a joint regulation of information duties of an entrepreneur and the obligatory content of* distance contracts and contracts negotiated outside business premises. In both cases, the entrepreneur is obliged, before concluding the contract or before the consumer makes a binding offer, to provide the consumer with the details specified in section 1820 al. 1. The contract must also include the details provided to the consumer before concluding the contract (section 1822).

The provision on consumer protection in distance contracting and contracts negotiated outside business premises does not extend to the contracts:

– for social services;
– for providing health care;
– for bets, games or lotteries;
– for a right to immovable property and lease of a flat;
– for tourist trip;
– for financial services under special acts;
– concluded through vending machines or automated shopping places;
– concluded by distance communication means operators via public telephones;
– concluded for the origin, change or termination of real property or lease of a flat;

– for supply of foods, drinks or other goods of common consumption delivered by standing suppliers into the consumer's house or residence;
– for transport of persons.

The legal regulation of the so-called distance contracts (contracts made in distance) reflects the development of the modern means of communication. An essential requirement for conclusion of the contract is to reach contractual accord. The means used by both parties to express their will and thus conclude the contract recognizable by third parties are not restricted in general. Therefore, there are a number of common tools used in presence of the persons negotiating (a face-to-face negotiation); also, a number of means enable negotiating between absent persons (typically employing the postal service). Basically, with consumer contracts, all means enabling distant communication can be utilized. Special attention is paid to some communication media in the Civil Code due to the fact that in their use a considerable risk of abuse against the consumer arises. Except contracts through letter writing, such means are included here that are operated by a businessman providing as his business activity one or more distance communication means and media – namely, non-addressed prints, addressed prints, type letters, advertising prints with an order print, catalogue, telephone attended by a service and telephone without service (automatic call device, audio text, radio, videophone, electronic mail, fax, etc.).

As consumers often are insufficiently equipped for using such means and facilities and in order to check the correctness of the relevant data, the law provides certain measures of protection through:

(1) the possibility of excluding the use of such means in distance communication;
(2) imposing a duty to the supplier to provide information as stated;
(3) stipulating the option for a consumer to withdraw from the contract in a statutory period:
   - Other specifying rules are given for some distance communication means. Such means of distance communication enabling individual acts may be used only when the consumer has not rejected their use. Automatic telephone systems without (human) attendance and faxes may be used only upon previous express consent of the consumer.
   - The proposition submitted by a distance communication means must contain the necessary information for conclusion of the contract under general contract terms provided by general part of the Civil Code and fundamental contractual terms as provided in the Part 8 of the Civil Code (depending on the type of the contract proposed – e.g., the subject and price in the sale contract). This information must be provided in a certain and intelligible manner with the regard to good morals and to protection of persons, namely, minors or consumers. The requirement of certainty of information concerns the content, intelligibility being a requirement for their expression. The Civil Code further defines the range of particularly necessary information by dividing it into two groups in relation to the time when it must be given to the consumer.

II. Contracts Negotiated Outside Business Premises

101. These are contracts concluded outside the spaces usual for the supplier's operation or anywhere else if the businessman has no permanent place to operate (e.g., pedlary). Consumer protection is based on his/her right to rescind the contract within various periods of time, the length of which is dependent on performing the goods or service delivery by the supplier and possibly on violation of the duty to inform. Not later than on the conclusion of contract the supplier is obliged to notify in writing the consumer about his/her right to withdraw from the contract. The written notification must state also the name of the person including his/her residence with whom this right must be claimed.

The consumer is entitled to withdrawing from the contract:

- within the period of fourteen days after the conclusion of the contract;
- within the period of one month after the conclusion of the contract unless the goods or service delivery by the supplier has been performed;
- within the period of one year and fourteen days after the conclusion of the contract unless the supplier has notified the consumer in writing about his right to rescind the contract.

III. Financial Services

102. Special consumer protection is given to consumer contracts relating to bank, payment or insurance services, contributory pension scheme, exchange of currencies, issuing electronic money and providing investment services or transactions on the market with investment instruments. This protection applies when such a contract is concluded exclusively by distance communication means. The protection includes: a special announcement before concluding the contract pursuant to section 1843, C.C.; the requirement of conformity of the content of the concluded contract with the information communicated before its concluding; the right to withdrawal from the contract with exceptions and consequences pursuant to sections 1846–1850. In the case of an expressly not-ordered financial service, no duties arise for the consumer.

As for the current regulation of consumer credit, *see* more paragraph number 118.

IV. Timesharing Contracts

103. Contracts for use of accommodation facilities for more than one period of time, or for other rights connected with it, including participation in an exchange system for such an accommodation and including the assistance of an entrepreneur when gaining such a right by payment or transfer are part of consumer contracts with a special regime concerning: the duty to inform before concluding the contract; the written form of the contract; the compulsory content of the contract; the language of the contract; options and periods of time (always of fourteen days duration) for withdrawal from the contract (sections 1852–1867).

Chapter 2. Sales

104. Purchase and sale is a legal relationship arising from a contract of sale. One party (the seller) is bound to hand over the subject of sale to the other party (the purchaser) who is bound to take it over and pay the purchase price. Both parties to a contract of purchase may comprise several subjects (e.g., an item is being sold or obtained through the sale by co-owners). The essential terms of a sale contract are a subject matter of sale and sale price:

(a) All things that are things in the legal sense and are in possession of the seller but are not *extra commercium* (e.g., things in exclusive possession of the State) can be subject to sale contract. The object of a sale contract may be determined individually, in kind, in bulk or in total. The object of a sale contract need not exist at the time of conclusion of the contract; sale of a future thing may be in question. Also an aleatory contract may be in question when the purchaser obliges himself/herself to pay the purchase price for things that will arise in the future regardless of whether expectations will come true and regardless of their amount and quality (e.g., purchase of future harvested crop). A part of a main thing may neither object of sale being not an independent thing under law, nor may be object of individual sale an accessory to a thing if determined by the possessor to use the thing together with the main thing, that is, by the time it has lost the character of an accessory.

(b) Price is a monetary consideration for the subject matter of a sale contract. It must be expressed in money; otherwise, there is no sale contract. The amount of sale price is given by agreement while respecting generally binding price regulations (if they exist) under the sanction of relative invalidity. For an agreement on the sale price to be certain at least, the form of its determination must be agreed upon. Maturity of obligation to pay sale price may be agreed as desired. Usually one of the following ways is used:
   - payment upon the delivery and receiving the subject matter of sale (typically for sale in shop);
   - following the delivery and receiving the object of sale contract (e.g., based on invoice) or possibly following ownership title transfer (after registration in the Land Registry);
   - prior to delivery and receiving the object of sale contract.

The mode of payment (in cash, by credit transfer) and non-recurring or instalment payment is governed by agreement.

A sale contract arises as soon as the parties have agreed upon its content. For a contract to be valid, written form is required only if the object of sale is a real property; otherwise, it may be concluded as desired.

The so-called accessory/collateral agreement may make a part of the sales contract. The Civil Code contains more detailed provisions for three of them:

- Retention of title, by which a general principle of transferring ownership title to property by taking the thing over is modified. It may be agreed upon sale of movables only, and the agreement must be concluded in writing. Its effect is that the purchaser obtains ownership right only upon full sale price payment.

- Preemption right, establishing a duty for the thing's owner, in case of his/her wish to alienate the thing (in the way as stated in the contract, or under law – by sale only), to offer an option to the former owner (the seller) to purchase it. Preemption right is of obligatory nature under law even though effects in rem may be agreed upon, but on the side of the purchaser only (preemption right does not pass on to heirs as a title and may not be transferred to another person). The agreement with effects in rem must be concluded in writing. Registration in the Land Registry is necessary for a preemption right with effects in rem to arise, and therefore, it can be concluded only in relation to real property registered in the Land Registry. If preemption right has been violated, the contract is not invalid, but the party entitled may claim to be offered the purchase of the thing by the assignee, or his/her preemption right will be preserved; that is, this assignee must offer him/her the thing if he/she wants to alienate it.
- Repurchase right, entitles the seller to demand from the purchaser to sell him/her back the sold thing after a certain time. The length of the time may be agreed upon; otherwise, repurchase right may be claimed only no later than one year after the delivery of the thing to the purchaser. In repurchase reserve, the person entitled may opt the term stated to decide to obtain back the thing sold. An alienation contract by which the repurchase right was violated is void.
- Repurchase reserve entitling the purchaser to sell back the item bought back by the seller within a certain time, as well as a number of other reserves and terms admitting the termination of legal relation arising from a sales contract (a better purchaser reserve, etc.).
- Test purchase is tied with the condition of the purchaser's confirmation of the purchase within a test period.
- Reservation of a better purchaser gives someone an option to make the contract with a purchaser with a better offer if he/she submits it within a specified period of time.
- The price clause makes it possible to adjust additionally the sale price taking the production costs into account.

§1. Sale of Movable Thing

105. Czech legislator used in the recent (but also in the former Civil Code 1964) legal regulation of sale contracts in the significant measure the United Nations Convention on Contracts for the International Sale of Goods – CISG). The Czech legal regulation of sale contracts is based on the main principles of CISG,[16] on the

16. Such as contract autonomy, informality etc.

rules of CISG and also on the style of interpretation. There are also the unified interpretation rules INCOTERMS 2010, which are important for the interpretation of contracts, because they take – if agreed between contract parties – priority over the legal rules.[17] The practice of CISG in the Czech law is newly summarized in one significant commentary.[18]

Rights and obligations of the parties to the contract in sale contract are both mutual and mutually conditioned as sale contract – this is a typical example of synallagmatic contracts. Usually, the following rights and obligations originate from a sales contract for the parties to the contract:

- The seller has a duty to perform properly the object of sale, that is, the duty to deliver the object of sale at the time as agreed by the parties. The moment of delivery is important for acquiring title to a movable thing. Along with an ownership right, acquiring a risk of accidental perishing and accidental deterioration of the sales object is passed on to the purchaser, unless agreed otherwise. If the purchaser acquired the ownership title even before, the seller owes the rights and duties of a bailee by the time the thing has been delivered (*see* explanation of bailment).
- The seller is bound to perform without unreasonable delays, but time of performance may be agreed on, too, or another term may be usual (*see* order sale). The seller is entitled to refuse to deliver the object of sale if the purchaser has not paid the price on time (unless agreed otherwise). If the object of sale is posted to the place of performance or place of destination, the purchaser is not bound to pay the price before he/she has the chance to look at the object of sale (necessary, usually, in a cash-on-delivery sale). The seller also bears the costs related to the sales object delivery (unless agreed otherwise) – namely, the measuring, weighing and packaging costs.
- The purchaser is bound to take over the subject of sale tendered properly and on time. If he/she is in delay with takeover, the seller may deposit the sale object in a public storage facility or in other bailment at the cost of the purchaser, or he/she may sell the object, after notifying the purchaser, at the cost of the purchaser. In case of perishable goods and lack of time, notification is not necessary.

It is a duty of the seller to notify the purchaser about the defects of the thing, if he/she is aware of them. This duty should be fulfilled at the moment of conclusion of the contract of sale. If a defect appears later that the purchaser was not notified about by the seller (who may not have known about it) and that existed at the time of delivery, the purchaser is entitled to:

17. Cf. Tichý, L. in: Švestka, J., Dvožák, J., Fiala, J. a kol. Občanský zákoník. Komentář. (Civil Code. Commentary), Svazek (Volume). V., Praha: Wolters Kluwer, a.s. 2014, s. (page) 723
18. Tichý, L. CISG (Úmluva OSN o smlouvách o mezinárodní koupi zboží – UN Convention on Contracts for the International Sale of Goods). 1. vydání. Praha: C. H. Beck, 2017, 412 s.

- remain a contractor and demand a discount from the agreed sale price, the amount of reduction corresponding with the nature and extent of the defect – the purchaser has this right regardless of the type of defect (both removable and non-removable);
- to rescind contract if the defect makes the thing unserviceable.

The defect that became apparent later is a defect that the thing had at the time of delivery; it is not a defect that was notified about by the seller. If the seller assured the purchaser that the thing had certain properties (namely, those demanded by the purchaser), or that the thing had no defects, and this assurance proves to be untrue, the purchaser may rescind the contract even if the defect does not make the thing unserviceable.

The defects must be reported by the purchaser without an unreasonable delay. Liability for defective products may be claimed in court only if the purchaser submitted objection to the seller within six months since taking possession of the thing and within three weeks if the defects involve fodder and six weeks if the defects involve animals. The purchaser can demand recovery of costs incurred due to defective performance. The purchaser may claim the recovery in court only if having notified the seller about them in the same terms stated for claiming defects. If the purchaser has claimed the right arising from liability for defects, his/her right to recovery of damages is not affected.

The legal relation arising from contract of sale is terminated by the usual ways of contract discharge, mainly by performance. In addition to this, a frequent reason for a contract discharge is withdrawal; consequences of a collateral agreement (e.g., resolutive conditions) may be employed, too.

§2. Sale of Immovable Thing

106. The contract on sale of immovables requires a written form (section 560, C.C.); this also applies to collateral provisions (*see* above) if property rights are established by them. Rights arising from a hidden defect of a structure firmly attached to the ground must be claimed within five years since the acquisition; otherwise, the court does not recognize them if they are protested by the seller.

I. Exchange (Barter) Contract

107. Exchange is a legal relationship arising from an exchange contract and by which the parties have both a right and an obligation to exchange mutually a thing for a thing. Purchase contract provisions will be applied as appropriate in such a manner that each party is considered as the supplier and the purchaser at the same time. Special provisions on consequences of deterioration or destruction of a thing may be found in sections 2184–2188, C.C.

Appropriate application of the sales contract provisions means that the provisions consistent with the character of the exchange contract will be used (e.g., the provision on purchase price will not be applied).

II. Sale of Goods in Shops

108. The provisions on the sale of goods in shops – regulating situations when a business (natural or artificial legal person) sells goods within its business activities – concentrate predominantly on the purchaser's protection and involve some kinds of sale and its consequences, quality and quantity rules and remedies for a non-conforming performance.

Among the particular types of sales, sale on order is explicitly regulated when such things are sold the nature of which requires so as well as items sold only exceptionally by the business. The businessman is obliged to procure the thing ordered within a term agreed, if it is not agreed on, then within a reasonable time, otherwise the ordering party is entitled to withdraw from the contract. By withdrawal, his/her right to recovery of damages is not affected.

Provisions concerning the consequences of taking over the thing a specification of the moment of acquiring ownership of the thing purchased, usually in case of mail-order sale and self-service sale are worth attention. Two exceptions to the general rule that the title is acquired upon taking possession of the thing by the purchaser are:

(1) mail-order sale when the purchaser acquires the title upon taking possession of the thing but at the place of delivery determined by him/her;
(2) self-service sale when the transfer of the title to the thing purchased occurs at the moment of paying the price for the chosen goods. By this moment, the purchaser may return the chosen goods to their original place (if the purchaser damages or destroys the chosen goods before acquiring the title, he is liable for damage under general provisions on liability for damage).

Performances that are not usually linked to the sale of a thing must be agreed on. These are situations when the purchaser demands special packaging (gift packaging, delivery of goods to his/her residence, etc.).

109. Liability for damage can be distinguished as:

(a) Liability for defects – arising from the seller's liability for the defects that the sold thing has after being taken by the purchaser. This liability does not relate to the things used if the defects are caused by their use or wear, or the things sold at lower prices if the price reduction was provided due to the defect in question.
(b) Warranty liability – liability for defects arising after taking possession of the thing by the purchaser. Under warranty liability, a warranty under law (the terms stipulated directly by law) and contractual warranty (arising from a contract or by accepting a one-sided declaration made in the certificate of guarantee the content of which may not be narrower to that stated under law) can be distinguished. Warranty under law applies to sale of goods that are not perishable or used. When products are sold in shops, it is presumed that the thing was faulty already when being received if the defect appears within six months

since the receipt. There is a special rule for consumer goods: if a defect appears within twenty-four months since the receipt, the purchaser is entitled to claiming a right from the defect.

III. Sale (Transfer) of the Enterprise

110. Under an enterprise sale contract, the seller obliges himself/herself to hand over to the purchaser an enterprise and to transfer title to the enterprise, and the purchaser obliges himself/herself to take over the obligations of the seller related to the enterprise and pay the sale price. The contract is required to have a written form only if the purchaser is recorded in the public register or if the enterprise includes a real estate.

The subject matter of sale is an enterprise, and the law does not require any particular items, rights or other values to be specified under the contract, employees, rights and obligations, intellectual property rights, etc.; the enterprise itself, or its part that is subject to the sale, must be individualized. An essential of the contract is the enterprise denoted, or its part, being subject to the sale, the obligation of the seller to hand over the enterprise to the purchaser and to transfer on him/her the title to the enterprise, and the purchaser's obligation to take over the seller's obligations related to the enterprise and to pay the selling price. As for determining the selling price, it must be taken into account that a subject matter of sale as a rule is an enterprise that is under operation and whose business assets constantly vary, while as a rule some time has run between conclusion of the contract and the instant when it has become effective. Basically, selling price is deemed to be stated by giving the sum of things, rights and obligations stated in the books of accounts of the enterprise sold upon the day of conclusion of the contract and based on other values stated in the contract, unless they are included in the accountancy. If the contract is to become effective on a later date, the purchase price sum will be changed in relation to the increase or reduction of assets accruing in the meantime.

Transfer of debts is governed by rules of assignment of claim under the Civil Code. For the assignment to be effective, a notice of assignment served on the debtor, or a proof of assignment by the seller, is required. Before this notice or proof, the debtor may perform his/her obligation to his/her original creditor, that is, the seller. In relation to transfer of debts and obligations, in the interests of legal certainty, the law imposes the seller to notice the debtors without delay on the respective transfer of debts on to the purchaser and to announce to the purchaser the obligations takeover to the respective creditors.

To protect the original owner's creditors, the creditors of the current enterprise owner – to raise an objection in court (actionability) within one month following the day when they were informed about the enterprise sale but no later than three years after the sale has been effective – may ask the court to rule that the obligation transfer by the seller upon the purchaser is most ineffective for them.

All the rights arising from industrial or other intellectual property involving business activities of the enterprise on sale are transferred by law on the purchaser, too. The transfer does not involve the rights of personal nature, which, according to the law, are non-transferable.

Based on the mandatory provisions, the rights and obligations arising from ownership of enterprise towards the enterprise employees are passed from the seller on to the purchaser. Rights and obligations of employees are specified closely under the Labour Code and employment contract.

The provisions related to enterprise sale as a whole apply also for the contracts under which a part of an enterprise, which is a separate organization unit, is sold.

If the seller is a person registered in the public Registry, the cogent stipulation of the Civil Code demands this sale be entered in the public Registry. In such a case, the seller will propose the filing of the respective entry. The collection of documents, making part of the Trade Registry, contains also a certificate about the sale of the enterprise or its part.

111. Donation (sections 2055–2078 C.C.) as a legal relationship arises by deed, by which the donor gratuitously gives or promises to give gratuitously something to the donee, and the donee accepts the gift or the promise of gift. Donation is not a unilateral juridical act. There is no donation if the property benefit is assigned without the will to make a deed of donation.

Elements of deed of donation are gratuitousness (lack of consideration) and free will. Gratuitousness means that the donee is not legally bound to provide consideration for the gift. There is no donation if the property benefit is assigned based on a legal obligation and not at free will (e.g., maintenance duty performing).

Donation deed generally does not require any specific form, unless the gift is given and taken at the moment of donating or if the donated thing is recorded in the public Registry. The respective deed must be made in writing.

Donation for the case of death (mortis causa) is usually considered to be bequest.

The donor's pledge to support the donee regularly is considered to be a gift, too; such a pledge passes to the donor's and the donee's heirs if it is expressly agreed upon.

The most important obligation and right of a donor is to provide gratuitous property performance to the donee. The donee has a respective right and obligation to accept the gift. The donor is also bound to notify about defect of the gift if he/she knows about them, when offering the donation. Otherwise, the donor is liable for the damage arisen from a defect of the donated thing and the donee may withdraw from the contract.

If the thing has a defect that the donor did not notify the donee about, the donee is entitled to return the thing but only if the defect had existed at the time of donation, and it did not occur later.

Donation as a legal relationship terminates due to general causes of obligation discharge, most often by performance.

A specific cause of termination of donation (or legal effects of donation) are:

- when the donor demands the gift be returned because the donee behaves to him/her and his/her family in a way that is contra bonus mores;
- or, when the donor demands the gift to be returned because he/she has fallen into poverty.

Chapter 3. Contract for Work

112. Contractual relationship, the purpose of which is a work to be performed, arises from a contract for work. This is a contract, by which one party (provider) obliges himself/herself to the other party (client) to provide work for this party at his/her own risk and for remuneration. The rise of the contract is bound to the agreement of contractual parties on fundamental essentials, such as determining the work, the remuneration and carrying out the work at the risk of the provider. The Civil Code prescribes no special form for this contract to be valid (however, general provisions state that a building – a real property – contract must be concluded in writing).

The work is defined as a kind of work in which the result is usually of a material character – based on producing, repairing or adjusting, or possibly destroying a thing – but it may have a non-material character, too. C.C. includes special provisions for:

- the making of a structure (section 2623 and subsequent ones) and for;
- a work with a non-material effect (section 2631 and subsequent ones).

The remuneration – price – may be determined by a contract.

The price may be agreed upon:

- by a fixed amount;
- the manner of determining the price may be agreed upon (e.g., according to the budget); or
- it may be estimated at least.

If the parties have expressly made a contract without determining the price, it applies that the price agreed upon is that which is paid for the same thing or, at least, a comparable work, at the time of the conclusion of the contract and in similar conditions.

A fundamental element of a contract is to carry out the work at one's own risk. It is up to the contractor how he/she will perform the work. He/she also bears the risk in case of such circumstances barring him/her from performing the contract as proper. The risk of damage to the work always lies with its owner. The title to the subject matter of the work when the work is being carried out is regulated in sections 2599–2603. The right in rem as the subject matter of the work is acquired by the client ordering the work by taking possession of the work. At that moment at the latest, the risk of damage to the work passes to him/her.

In all cases of contracts for work, the parties to the contract have the following rights and obligations:

- The provider is bound to perform the work according to the contract. This obligation comprises a number of partial elements, including the issues of who is supposed to carry out the work, what material will be used, in what way, in what manner and in what time period.

- An essential duty of the client is to pay the remuneration to the provider. This remuneration must be provided in the place as agreed by the parties. Unless agreed otherwise, this place will be the ordering provider's residence. The remuneration for the work is payable as a rule after the work has been performed (a different agreement is possible). If the work is to be performed in parts, or if performing the work is very costly, the provider is entitled to demand a down payment as appropriate at the time when the work is being carried out. The provider has the right to the down payment as agreed even if the work has not been performed, if he/she was willing to carry out the work but he/she was frustrated by circumstances on the part of the client (the provider is bound to include what he/she has saved by non-performing the whole work, what he/she has earned in some other way, or what earnings he/she purposefully missed).
- The provider is bound to notify the client without delay about the drawbacks of the material delivered by him/her that prevents the provider from doing the work. The provider is bound in the same way when the client demands the work be done according to unsuitable instructions. In such a case, the provider is entitled to interrupting the work until the imperfections are rectified. If the client demands the work to be carried out, the provider is entitled to demanding such an order to be made in writing. If the work is carried out with unsuitable materials or according to unsuitable instructions from the client, the client does not have any rights from the imperfections of the work arisen in this way.

The provider may withdraw from the contract if cooperation of a client was inevitable to carry out the work and if the client was given a reasonable time for doing so, and nevertheless the client did not provide such cooperation. The client may withdraw from the contract if the work apparently will not be carried out on time, or will not be carried out properly, or if the provider does not go on working even if given an additional time.

The death of the client does not itself terminate the contract; however, it might cause the termination of the legal relationship due to the nature of the agreement or the purpose of the work (e.g., in ordering one's own portrait).

The death or loss of the provider's special personal abilities on which the work depends results in termination of the legal relationship only if the performance of the work depends on special abilities of the provider.

If the subject matter of the work is a thing and the client does not take possession of the work without unnecessary delay when the work was supposed to be carried out, or after having been informed about the completion of the work, the provider may sell the work at the expenses of the client. The work has a defect if it is not in accordance with the contract. The client's rights from a defective performance are dealt with similarly as in provisions about the sale contract. The client is obliged to declare the defects of the work without unnecessary delay when he/she has found them out; if he/she does not do that within two years since the work was taken over the court will not adjudicate the right to protesting the provider's delay. If the provider guarantees the quality of the work, the provisions of the C.C. are similarly applied.

General provisions on the contract for the work are applied to contracts for modification of a real estate and for making, repairing and modifying a structure. An exception is special provisions on:

- risk of danger to a thing;
- right to billing if the damage is determined with a reference to the real amount of the work and other costs;
- checking the progress made in carrying out the work;
- hidden obstacles;
- reception of the structure; and
- defects of the structure.

The work with an immaterial result has a special regulation concerning: the procedure when carrying out the work; delivery and receipt of the work; an option of the provider to give the result of his/her activities to other persons.

These provisions also regulate the result of activities carried out pursuant to the provision on public promise (a work in tender).

Chapter 4. Healthcare

113. With the contract for medical treatment, the provider undertakes towards the principal to take care, within the limits of his/her job or the object of his/her enterprising, of the health of the person who is being treated regardless of that being the principal or a third person (sections 2636–2651). The principal may be someone different from the person who is being treated; the person who is being treated and is not the principal may refuse the treatment; by his/her refusal the obligation is discharged.

The conceptual element of the obligation is not payment as a substantial part of the medical treatment is paid from the public health insurance and therefore the principal is obliged to pay the provider a remuneration only if it has been agreed upon.

Medical treatment includes an act, an examination or a piece of advice and all other services that are directly concerning the person who is being treated and that are guided by an effort to improve or preserve his/her health condition; it is not an activity consisting only in sale or another transfer of drugs.

The provider is usually only liable for professionality of the act, not for achieving the result. For this reason, the Civil Code imposes an information duty on the provider when the provider clearly explains to the person who is being treated (or to his/her legal representative) the intended examination and the suggested treatment; after the respective examination, the provider explains to the person who is being treated his/her health condition and the further treatment; if required by the person who is being treated the provider gives him/her the explanation in writing. If this put the health condition of the person who is being treated partly or completely into danger, the full explanation may be given additionally when the danger is not imminent.

For any act within the medical treatment, the consent of the person who is being treated is required, unless provided by the law that it is not necessary. The refusal of the consent is confirmed in writing by the person who is being treated at the request of the provider. Either party confirms at the request of the other party the extent of the given consent.

According to the contract, the provider proceeds with professional care and in conformity with the rules of his/her profession (*lege artis* care) and is liable for fulfilling his/her duties; different provisions are not taken into account. If the medical treatment is provided in a healthcare institution, a social services institution or another similar institution which is not run by the contractual party, the person who is being treated must be informed in time who is the provider and that the runner of the institution is not a contractual party.

The provider keeps records of the medical treatment which must be clear about the health condition of the person who is being treated and about the provider's activities including the papers evidencing correctness of these data to the extent needed for providing a proper medical treatment. The provider will keep the records for such a period of time as it is needed for providing professional care and he/she always makes a record of the person who has examined them. At the request of the person who is being treated, the provider will enable him/her, without unnecessary delay, to examine the records kept about him/her and will enable him/her to make extracts, transcriptions or copies, or he/she themselves will give him/her an extract, a transcription or a copy after being paid an appropriate remuneration. The records cannot be made accessible to another person without the consent of the person who is being treated unless the law provides otherwise; if the records also include information about a third person, it cannot be made accessible without their consent. The information about the person who is being treated may be communicated by the provider only in an anonymous form and only to scientific or statistics institutions and in conformity with legally set conditions.

Chapter 5. Licences

114. With a licence contract, the provider provides the acquirer with authorization to exercise the right to intellectual property (licence) to the agreed limited or unlimited extent and the acquirer undertakes, unless provided otherwise, to give the provider a remuneration (sections 2358–2389). The contract must be in writing if the licence is exclusive or if the licence is to be recorded in the respective public register (licence for the subject matter of industrial property recorded in the public register becomes effective towards third persons by being recorded in this register). The licence may be:

– an exclusive one;
– a non-exclusive one.

The provider may provide a third person with an authorization included in the licence completely or partially only if this has been agreed upon in the licence contract, and with the consent of the provider the acquirer may assign the licence to a third person (completely or partially).

Providing a licence is usually for payment and gratuitousness must be expressly agreed upon. If the amount of the remuneration or the manner of its determination have not been agreed upon, the licence contract is still valid if it follows from the parties' acting when concluding the contract that they have wished to make a contract for value even without determining the amount of the remuneration; in such a case, the acquirer will pay the provider a remuneration in such an amount that is usual at the time of the conclusion of the contract under similar contractual conditions and for such a right, or if the parties have expressly agreed upon gratuitousness.

The legal relationship between the provider and the acquirer is terminated in the same manner as obligations are usually discharged, especially being regulated the termination on the basis of a discharge of a licence agreed for an indeterminate term.

The general regulation of licence is linked with three groups of special provisions:

(1) for the licence for subject matters protected by the Copyright Act;
(2) for the publisher's contract of licence;
(3) for neighbouring rights to copyright and for the right of the database creator.

Ad (a) With the contract, the author provides the acquirer with authorization to use the copyrighted work in an original or processed or otherwise altered form, in a certain manner or in all manners of use, and to a limited or an unlimited extent; the acquirer is obliged to make use of the licence for the copyrighted work unless provided otherwise. The licence may be limited to particular manners of the use of the work; the manners of the use of the work may be limited by the extent, especially as far as the amount, the place or the time are concerned. If the acquirer does not make use of the exclusive licence at all or if he/she makes use of it insufficiently and due to that the legitimate interests of the author are considerably affected, the author may withdraw from the contract but only when he/she has asked the acquirer to make use of the licence sufficiently within an appropriate period of time since the appeal being served and the acquirer has failed to make use of the licence sufficiently in spite of that appeal. The author may also withdraw from the contract when a copyrighted work, which has not been published yet, does not correspond to his/her beliefs any more, and by publishing it his/her legitimate personal interests would be considerably affected in a negative way. By the death of a natural person or the termination of a legal person provided with the licence, the rights and duties from the licence contract are transferred to their legal successor. The licence contract may exclude such a transfer of rights and duties to a legal successor.

By the licence contract for publishing the author provides the acquirer with a licence to reproduce and distribute a copyrighted work of a literary, musical-dramatical, musical, visual or photographic nature, or expressed in a manner resembling photography, if it is not the use of a copyrighted work by performing artists. The acquirer will provide the author, before publishing the copyrighted work, with an appropriate period of time to carry out minor creative changes of his/her work which will not bring about inappropriate expenses on the part of the acquirer and which will not alter the nature of the work (the author's proofreading). If the proofreading is not enabled, the author may withdraw from the contract.

Ad (c) Provisions on licences for subject matters protected by the Copyright Act, with specified exceptions, are used similarly for artistic performances, sound recordings, audiovisual recordings and radio or television broadcasting. These provisions are used adequately, also with some divergences, for databases that are subject to the special right of the creator of databases.

Chapter 6. Loans

§1. Loan for Consumption

115. Legal relationship arises from a loan contract in which one party (the creditor) transfers the things stated in kind to the other party (the debtor) and the debtor obliges himself/herself to return the things of the same kind after lapse of a fixed period. Fundamental essentials of the contract are handing over a thing, stating the generic thing in kind (unlike in borrowing and lease), temporality of the relationship and the duty to return the thing of the same kind. As a rule, the subject matter of a loan is money as an instrument of payment.

Basically, loans are classified according to the distinction into monetary and non-monetary loans.

The creditor is obliged to hand over the subject of loan, and the debtor is bound to return the things of the same kind in the same amount and quality as he/she borrowed, at the time stated. With a non-financial loan, parties may agree that the debtor will be bound to return a larger amount of the things or of a better quality. With a financial loan or a loan in securities, the debtor is bound to pay interests only if they have been agreed on. The amount of interests is not specified by law. Opposite to interests for delay, the loan interest should be understood as a payment for use of the surety borrowed. If the interests were agreed on in an inappropriate amount, the agreement will be void due to inconsistency with good morals.

If the contract does not specify the time of returning the loan, it is necessary to discharge the contract; if not specified the period of notice of discharge is six weeks. If the interests are not agreed upon, the debtor may pay off the loan without a notice.

§2. Loan for Use

116. Loan for use, called 'borrowing' in Czech law, is a legal relationship arising by contract under which the lender leaves the thing to the borrower for a gratuitous temporal usage. Significant elements of this contract are handing over of the thing for use, gratuitousness and temporality. The objects of borrowing are only the things stated individually, and these things must be returned to the lender without impairing its substance. Borrowing differs from loan by the object and by gratuitousness from lease.

The lender is bound to hand over the thing to the borrower. If special rules are to be observed in the use of the thing borrowed – usually, if the use is governed by instructions for use or is regulated by a technology standard – the lender is bound to notify the borrower about it unless the rules are generally known.

The borrower is entitled and bound to use the thing as proper according to the purpose agreed under the contract and if the purpose has not been agreed upon, for the purpose the thing usually serves. The borrower is bound to protect the thing from damage, loss or destruction. The thing borrowed may be handed over for use to another person only with the consent of the borrower. The duty of the borrower is also to return the thing borrowed either after extinction of the legal relationship or even before lapse of time agreed for the borrowing as soon as he/she no longer needs it. This duty is the same when, according to law, the lender has demanded returning the thing even before lapse of the time stated.

The Civil Code establishes liability for damage for the lender, arising from the fact that he/she did not duly inform the borrower about special rules for the use of the thing or defects of the thing.

The termination of the legal relation arising from the borrowing contract arises for a number of reasons, both common for all types of contracts and specific.

Common termination arises in response to the purpose of borrowing, that is, lapse of the time agreed for the borrowing and performance of the purpose of borrowing. A specific reason for termination of legal relationship arises from the demand of the lender to return the thing before lapse of the time agreed because the borrower does not use the thing as proper or uses it inconsistently with the purpose to which it serves. Another reason for termination is when the borrower lets another person use the thing without the lender's consent.

The borrower may return the thing prematurely; however, if this caused the borrower any difficulties then it may be done only with his/her consent.

Rights of the borrower and the lender, if they have not been claimed in court after three months since the returning of the thing, will not be recognized by the court when protested by the other party.

A special kind of giving the use of a thing to another person is precarium (sections 2189–2192, C.C.). This relationship arises by the lender's giving gratuitously a thing to use without determining the period of use or the purpose of use. In such a case the lender may demand returning the thing at his/her will.

§3. Credit

117. The contract for credit is a consensual contract on the basis of which the creditor undertakes to provide the debtor, at his/her request and for his/her benefit, with a certain amount of financial means and the debtor undertakes to return the provided financial means and to pay the interests. The principal aim of this obligation is the creditor's profit represented by the interests.

The use of the credit may be restricted to a particular purpose.

The debtor will exercise the right to providing money within a period determined in the contract; otherwise, the right may be exercised if the obligation from the contract persists. The creditor will provide money at the request of the debtor within the period of time determined in the request, and if the period is not determined in the request then without unnecessary delay. The money may be returned before the agreed time; the interests are then paid only for the period since returning the money.

If the money is used for another purpose than the agreed one, or if the use of the money for the agreed purpose becomes impossible, the creditor may withdraw from the contract and demand returning the gained money together with the interests.

§4. Consumer Credit

118. Since 1 January 2011 till the end of 2016, the Act No. 145/2010 Coll. on consumer credit has been in force. The act implemented rules of European Communities into the Czech contract law (Directive of European Parliament and Council 2008/48/ES from 23 April 2008) regulating rights and duties relating to deferred payment, loan, credit or other financial services of similar kind provided or promised to the consumer by the creditor or the broker. The most important rights of the consumer, when being provided with the consumer credit, include the information duty the breach of which is sanctioned by invalidity, the creditor's duty to assess in advance the consumer's ability to pay off the credit, the establishing of the annual percentage rate of the credit costs, the possibility to withdraw from the contract without giving a reason within fourteen days since the concluding of the consumer credit, the possibility for the consumer as well as the creditor to terminate anytime the consumer credit contract made for indefinite period, rules for tied consumer credits and the possibility to pay off the consumer credit prematurely and restriction of the right to compensation of credit costs and premature payoff.

By the end of 2016, the new quality of consumer protection is also given to contracts of consumer credit. This type of contracts is newly regulated by the Act. No. 257/2016 Coll., Consumer Protection Act. This regulation introduced into the Czech contract law the current EU dimension of consumer protection, mainly against usurious practices of providers of loans and credits. It gives to the consumers the larger possibility of withdrawal from the contract. Newly, when the contract enables the provider´s usurious practices, is considered to be void. The act establishes also the legal limitation of amount of fees negotiated in the credit or loan consumer contract.

Chapter 7. Contract of Employment

119. The contract of employment is only mentioned in the Civil Code as a concept; the whole legal regulation of the contract of employment is included in the Labour Code (Act No. 262/2006 Col.).

Chapter 8. Lease Contracts

§1. General Provisions

120. Under lease contract, a party (the lessor) lets a thing for temporary use to another party (the lessee) for a rent over a fixed period when the lessee may use the thing. The lessor is obliged to pass the leased thing to the lessee in a condition fit for the agreed use, unless agreed otherwise and is liable for an undisturbed use of the thing for the period of the lease.

It is possible to lease both an immovable thing and a non-consumable movable thing, or a part of an immovable thing, or a thing that will be created in the future. If a thing is recorded in the public register, it is also possible to record the lease right in the register at the motion of the owner or the lessee with the consent of the owner.

The lessee is obliged to pay the rent fixed in the contract, or else the amount of rent as usual at the time of conclusion of the contract, taking into account the value of the leased thing and the manner of its use. However, a lease contract is valid even if the contract does not fix the amount of the rent. If a rent is stated in statutory provisions, such regulation applies.

The lessee is obliged to use the thing as a proper keeper for the agreed or usual purpose; he/she is obliged to inform the lessor of the defects that the lessor is obliged to rectify. The lessee carries out ordinary maintenance during the lease. A sublease may be created by the lessee only with the consent of the lessor in a form identical with the form of the lease contract. For the period of the sublease, the lessee is liable to the lessor for the actions of the sublessee.

By changing the title to a subleased thing, the rights and duties of the lessor are transferred to a new owner. Details are included in sections 2221–2224, C.C.

The lease contract terminates upon expiry of the period fixed in the contract, unless the parties agree otherwise. If the lessee continues to use a thing after the end of the lease period and the lessor does not ask him/her to hand over the thing it applies that the lease contract has been renewed under the existing conditions for the period of one year if the lease period was longer than one year; in the case of a shorter period, it is for the originally agreed period. The lease contract concluded for an indefinite period may be terminated only by giving notice of termination, unless the parties come to an agreement. In the case of lease of real estate, a three-month notice is to be given; and in the case of movable things, a one-month notice shall apply.

If a thing perishes, the lease is ended. If it perishes partially, the lessee is entitled to a rent discount or he/she may discharge the lease without a period of notice. The lease agreed for a definite period may be discharged by the parties only if the discharge reasons and the period of notice have been agreed upon.

If a thing becomes, without the lessee's influence, unusable for the agreed or usual purpose the lessee is entitled to discharge the contract without a period of notice. The lessor, too, has the right to discharge the contract under conditions specified in section 2228 if there is a danger of excessive wear or destruction of the thing by being used.

The lessor has the right to de-strain movable things of the lessee situated on or in the thing to cover costs of his/her claim.

§2. Lease of Flats and Houses

121. In Czech Civil Code, the regulation of the lease of flats and houses establishes special provisions in relation to the general provisions on a lease contract.

Lease of a flat (apartment) arises on the basis of relevant lease contract under which the lessor lets the lessee use the flat in return for payment of rent, either for a definite period or without fixing the period of use.

Czech civil law includes a specific regulation for cooperative flats (section 2240 C.C., sections 741–747 Commercial Corporation Act No. 90/2012 Coll). In the case of a cooperative flat, the relevant lease contract between the housing cooperative and its member may only be concluded under the terms laid down in the statutes of such cooperative. The member of a housing cooperative has a right, among others, to conclude a contract for the lease of a cooperative flat for an indefinite term if he/she fulfils the conditions of the law and the statutes, and a right to have such a rent determined that only includes purposeful expenses for the administration of flats including expenses for repairs, modernization, and reconstruction of the respective houses and a long-term contribution to the repairs of and investments into these flats. If the cooperative share is a part of the community property, a right to joint use of the flat arises. If one of the spouses is an exclusive member of the housing cooperative, both spouses have a derived joint right of lease to the flat.

In the case of service flats tied with the performance of work, the lessee's rights may be limited (sections 2297–2299, C.C.).

Some special rules hold for flats specially adjusted for the handicapped (sections 2300–2301 C.C.).

The contract for lease of a flat requires a written form but the lack of it cannot be protested by the lessor.

Unless otherwise provided by the law, rent is agreed on conclusion of the lease contract, or a change of rent is agreed during the lease relationship by agreement between the lessor and the lessee. If the rent has not been negotiated by agreement, the lessor has a right, for new leases, to have a rent usual at the time and in that place. The parties may agree upon a regular increase of the rent; if they do not do so or do not exclude increasing the lessor may demand an increase of the rent up to the amount of the locally comparable rent (more in sections 2248–2253).

The method of calculation of amounts (charges) for suppliers and services relating to use of a flat and the manner of their payment is laid down in other statutory provisions.

A flat may be jointly leased by two or more persons. Joint lessees shall have equal rights and obligations. In a cooperative flat, a joint lease may only be established between spouses.

If, during their marriage, spouses, or one of them, become(s) the lessee of a flat, or if the lessee of the flat concludes marriage, a joint lease of the flat by the spouses is established (sections 745 C.C.). The same applies to registered partnership (section 3020). Specific regulation is stated in the case of joint lease of the cooperative flat by the spouses (*see* above). Between the registered partners, no joint lease of the flat or the cooperative flat arises, but a partner has the right to use the flat leased by the other partner for the period of validity of the partnership.

The lessee has a right to keep a pet in the flat under the conditions set by law (section 2258).

The lessee has a right (an exception to the general rule on sublease – *see* above) to sublet the flat to another person if he is a permanent resident in the flat; otherwise he/she does not have this right.

The lessee has a right to accept anyone to his/her household but he/she is obliged to inform the lessor about that. The lessor has a right to reserve his/her consent with accepting a new member to the lessee's household except for a close person or cases worth of special consideration. The lessee is also obliged to inform about the reduction of the members of the household. By the death of the lessee, the lease passes to a member of the lessee's household under the conditions specified in section 2279. If this does not happen the rights and duties from the lease pass to the heirs of the lessee and both the lessor and the lessee may discharge the lease within three months with a two-month length of notice.

The lease of the flat terminates by a written agreement between the lessor and the lessee, by a written notice of termination or by another form stipulated by law.

The notice must be in writing and the lessor will inform the lessee about the right to protest the notice and to suggest its re-examination by the court; otherwise, the notice is invalid. The lease of flat is protected; the lessor may give notice of termination to the lessee only for the reasons stated by statute or law (section 2288 C.C.). The law distinguishes reasons for the notice of termination given by the lessor regardless of the agreed period of time and reasons for the notice of termination of the lease agreed only for an indefinite term. The lessee may, within two months since being served the notice, file a motion in court to have rightfulness of the notice re-examined.

The lessees may agree on an exchange of flats with the consent of the lessors.

§3. Lease of Business Premises (Space)

122. Under specific rules of C.C., the lease of business premises (space) is regulated. Under these rules, the lease arises in the case of the use of the leased premises for the purpose of business.

The purpose of the lease cannot be changed if it brought about worsening of the conditions of the premises or if an unreasonable harm occurred. The lessee may assign the lease in writing when transferring his/her business activities to another person if the lessor previously made a written consent with it. The lease may be discharged in cases and by manners set in sections 2308–2314.

§4. Lease of a Means of Transport (Special Rules)

123. The essential provision of this contract type stipulates that the lessor obliges himself/herself to leave a means of transport for a temporal use of the lessee, and the lessee obliges himself/herself to pay the rental fee. It is a relationship of lease, contrary to the means of transport operation, whereby the carrier obliges himself/herself to transport load and to carry out one or more trips for this purpose, and the carrier provides the staff and fuel to the means of transport. This provision determines fundamental terms of the contract as follows:

- the parties to the contract denoted: the lessor's means of transport and the lessee's means of transport;
- the obligation of the lessor to pass on the means of transport and respective documents;
- the means of transport denoted, which is a matter of interest;
- temporality of the means of transport used;
- the obligation of the lessee to pay the charge for using the means of transport after termination of the use; if the period is longer than three months, it is to be paid at the end of each month.

The lessee will make an insurance for the means of transport if it has been agreed so.

The lessor will reimburse the lessee for all the cost of the maintenance; this right may be claimed within three months, otherwise it terminates.

The right to use the means of transport terminates upon the lapse of term for which the contract has been concluded, or by destroying the means of transport.

§5. Accommodation

124. Accommodation under the Czech Civil Code is a legal relationship in which the accommodator (e.g., an owner or a manager of a hotel) is obliged to provide the ordering person with a temporal accommodation for the time agreed or for the time arising from the purpose of accommodation in the facilities assigned for this purpose (hotel, hostel, lodging house, etc.) and to provide performance related to the accommodation, while the ordering person (the accommodated person) is bound to pay the price to the accommodator within the terms as stated by accommodation rules.

The accommodation is provided under contract, the essentials of which are an agreement of the place and manner of accommodation and a statement of the period of accommodation. The price will be determined by accepting the proposed price determined by the accommodator as stated in the rules of accommodation.

Regarding the intent to provide temporal (short-term) accommodation, this relationship differs from lease of flats and lease of dwelling spaces in facilities intended for permanent dwelling.

The accommodated person undertakes to pay the accommodator for the accommodation and related services within the period set by the accommodation rules or within a usual period.

The accommodator is liable to the accommodated person for damage to things brought in by the accommodated person (sections 2946–2949). The accommodated person may, for the purpose of reducing the risk of damage to the things brought in, place money and other valuables to special custody of the accommodator.

The accommodated person may discharge the contract before the expiry of the agreed period of time. The accommodator may discharge the contract before the expiry of the agreed period of time without an advanced notice if the accommodated person, despite being warned, seriously breaches duties from the contract or good manners.

Chapter 9. Tenure (A Special Kind of Lease)

125. Unlike a simple lease contract, the tenure giver (lessor) gives the tenant (user) a thing for temporary use and consumption (taking fruits from the thing) and the tenant undertakes to pay a tenure rent or to provide a proportionate part of the fruits (yield) from the thing.

If the rented thing is recorded in the public register, the tenure may be recorded there, too, if suggested by the owner of the thing or, with his/her consent, by the tenant.

The thing cannot be passed to another person for use or consumption and the economic purpose of the thing or the manner of use cannot be changed without the lessor's consent; otherwise, the lessor may terminate the lease without an advance notice.

The tenant has a right to a rent discount, rent pardoning or lease discharge without an advanced notice if the lessor does not rectify an imperfection to which he/she is liable and if the yield falls under half of the usual yield, or the yield is very small.

The tenure for an indefinite term may be terminated within the six months period of notice so that it should end by the expiry of the tenure year. If the contract has been in writing, the notice of termination must also be in writing. A rebuttable presumption applies that the tenure year lasts since 1 October till 30 September in the case of agricultural tenure and one calendar year in other cases of tenure.

If the stock and equipment were rented together with the thing, the lessee will keep individual parts and will renew the stock as a proper keeper. However, if the lessee undertakes to return the stock and equipment at an agreed price he/she may freely dispose of it. For claims against the lessor, the lessee has a security interest in the stock and equipment; this right cannot be exercised if the lessee provides the lessor with another kind of security.

§1. Agricultural Tenure (Lease of a Land)

126. The subject matter of agricultural tenure is an agricultural or forest land. The contract need not be concluded in writing. The tenure rent is paid once a year in arrears, always on 1 October at the latest. The tenure for an indefinite term may be discharged within a one-year period of notice. If the lessee becomes physically incapable to farm the land, he/she may always discharge the tenure with a three-month advance notice. If the lessee dies, the same rule applies to his/her heirs but the notice must be delivered within six months since the lessee's death.

§2. Lease of an Enterprise

127. With a contract for lease of enterprise, the lessor obliges himself/herself to pass his/her enterprise on to the lessee in order for the lessee to operate and manage it independently at his/her own cost and risk and to obtain the respective benefit. The lessee obliges himself/herself to pay rent to the lessor.

The subject matter of the enterprise lease contract is an enterprise as a set of material, personal and non-material elements of entrepreneurship with a reservation that these are things, rights and other property values that belong to the lessor and serve the leased enterprise operation or they should serve, due to their nature (*see* section 502).

The lessee's duties are as follows:

- to operate the leased enterprise with reasonable care;
- not to change the subject matter of the business operated in the leased enterprise without the lessor's consent.

A special provision concerns the transfer of rights and obligations (including rights and duties arising from labour relations) that are attached to the enterprise leased, from the lessor to the lessee. This transfer occurs simultaneously with the contract becoming effective, that is, upon publication of the contract in the public Registry, or otherwise upon the effectiveness of the contract.

The enterprise lessor is obliged without unnecessary delay to inform the current creditors on the obligations takeover and on the debts transfer on the enterprise lessee. If recoverability of a debt is worsened by the lease, the creditor may claim ineffectiveness of the contract in relation to him/her within one or three months (section 2354).

The termination of an enterprise lease has, as provided by law, the following effects for the parties' relationship:

- on the day of the termination of the lease, the claims-debts connected with the enterprise pass to the lessor, but and only those debts that he/she knew or must have known about;
- if the creditor has not given his/her consent to the assumption of the debt by the lessor, it is the lessee who is liable for paying the debt;
- the transfer of claims is governed by provisions on assignment of claims;
- the lessee will notify the creditors and debtors about the termination of the lease; the lease termination must also be made public.

Chapter 10. Mandate Contracts

128. The aim and subject matter of this category of contracts is to procure a thing for the mandator by another person (the mandatary). These include generally formulated types of contracts such as an order in the narrower sense but also procuring specific issues such as forwarding or business representation.

§1. Mandate

129. Contract of mandate is a contract in which the mandatary obliges himself/herself to carry out some activity for the mandator. The object of the contract may thus be extensive, involving a juridical act (e.g., filing a case with a State authority) as well as a factual activity (e.g., auxiliary acts in preparation of a negotiation, which is the main object of a contract). Gratuitousness is not an essential of a mandate contract; the mandatary is entitled to remuneration if it has been agreed upon or if it is usual (e.g., a mandate of the given advocate within his professional activities).

The contract of mandate is closely related to the institute of agency, usually in the case of agency under procuration.

The contract arises upon agreement of the parties on the subject matter and possibly the remuneration if its providing would not be as of ordinary, usually in regard to the mandator's profession (e.g., an advocate). Parties to the contract of mandate are the mandator and the mandatary.

The mandatary is obliged:

– to procure a thing or carry out another activity consistent with the subject matter of contract while bound to act according to his/her abilities and knowledge;
– to observe the mandator's instructions – he/she may divert only if necessary for the interests of the mandator, and he/she is not able to obtain his/her consent on time; any other diversion from instruction is a violation of obligation of mandate, and therefore, the mandatary is liable for damage that might arise;
– to carry out the mandate in person; if the mandatary entrusts the mandate to a third person, he/she is liable just as if he/she carried out the mandate himself/herself, but if the mandator agreed to mandatary appointment of a deputy or if the appointment of the deputy was inevitable, the mandatary is liable merely for faults in selecting a deputy;
– to report completely, if required, about the course of the mandate performance and to transfer all benefits arising from the mandate performed on the mandator;
– to render an account after the mandate performance.

The mandator is obliged:

– to provide the mandatary, if required, with all appropriate means necessary for performing the mandate;

- to reimburse all necessary and beneficial costs incurred to the mandatary even if the result failed to come; at the request of the mandatary the mandator will make a deposit for these costs;
- to recover damage, including the faultless one arising in relation to the mandate performance (with the restricted scope in case of an accidental damage);
- to provide remuneration (only if agreed on or if it is common); the mandator is so obliged even if the result failed to come, unless procedure failure has been caused by the mandatary's breach of duty.

The legal relationship between the mandator and the mandatary terminates, as appropriate, pursuant to the provision on full agency extinction, that is by performing the act, by revoking the mandate, by repudiation by the mandatary or by the mandatary's or the mandator's death. The mandatary may not revoke the mandate until the end of the calendar month following the month in which the notice of termination was served. If this happens before procuring the matter, the mandatary shall compensate the mandator for the damage incurred. Upon termination by repudiation, the mandator is bound to reimburse the mandatary for the costs incurred before the repudiation, the damages and, if possible, for a part of the remuneration appropriate to the work done.

The provisions on mandate are applied appropriately also to the duty arisen from the contract or from the law to procure a matter for another person.

§2. Agency

130. Agency is a special type of mandate by which the agent undertakes for an interested person to broker the conclusion of a certain contract with another person and the interested person undertakes to pay brokerage.

If it is a contract for value, the brokerage is payable on the day of the conclusion of the brokered contract, or on the fulfilment of a condition; if procuring an opportunity to conclude a contract was agreed upon as the aim of the contract, the brokerage is payable on the procuring of the opportunity. The brokerage may also be agreed upon to be paid after another person's duty from the brokered contract has been fulfilled. It is presumed that the brokerage includes remuneration for the costs of the agency. The broker is entitled to remuneration for the costs incurred by the agency if no brokerage has been agreed upon. The broker is not entitled to brokerage or remuneration for the costs, if, in contradiction of the contract, he/she also acted for another party. The broker is also entitled to brokerage if the contract has been concluded or performed after the termination of an obligation from the contract of agency.

An obligation terminates if the contract has not been concluded within an agreed period of time. If the time has not been agreed upon, the obligation may be cancelled by either party notifying the other party.

§3. Undisclosed Mandate

131. This is a specific type of agency contract under the Civil Code. Under the basic stipulation of the Civil Code, a commissionary agent obliges himself/herself to procure a business matter for the principal in his/her own name but at his/her cost, and the principal obliges himself/herself to pay him/her for it. No written form is prescribed for this type of contract. Fundamental parts of a contract with a commissionary agent include:

- the parties to the contract: the commissionary agent and the principal;
- the subject matter of the contract, that is procuring a business matter;
- the commission agent's acting in his/her own name but at the cost of the principal;
- the payment.

In relation to its content, the contract with a commissionary agent has a number of identical features with the contract of agency because its subject matter is to arrange certain business matters; one essential difference is that the mandatary acts on behalf of the mandator, while the commissioner acts in his/her own name. The brokerage contract must be distinguished from that, too, because its feature is not the final arrangement of a matter (e.g., a regular conclusion of a certain contract) but only arranging an opportunity for the party interested in making a contract with a third party. This makes it substantially different from a business agency contract where this activity is permanent.

In arranging the matter, the commission agent, while exercising necessary reasonable care, is bound to act according to the principal's instructions from which he/she may divert only in cases stipulated by the law. He/she is also bound to protect his/her principal's interests (that he/she is aware of and that are related to the matter arranged) and inform him/her about all circumstances that might influence changes of the principal's orders, including the duty to inform the principal on arranging the given matters in the manner stipulated in the contract.

The commissionary agent is also bound to employ other persons in performing the contract where he/she would be unable to perform the obligation himself/herself.

The matter agreed is arranged by the commissionary agent himself/herself; therefore, he/she is liable for the contracts concluded in his/her own name, even though at the cost of his/her principal. Therefore, no rights and liabilities arise for the principal towards third parties as a result from the commissionary agent's acts. Third parties are in contractual relationship to the commissionary agent only.

If the person with whom the commissionary agent concluded the contract has not performed the contract, the principal may not claim this from the agent. The commissionary enforces such a performance from a third person. The right corresponding to this may be transferred by the commissionary to the principal if he/she agrees with that.

Regarding the essence of the contract with a commissionary agent, a special stipulation is contained in law involving transfer of the title to the things through a sale contract concluded by a commissionary agent in his/her own name and at his/her principal's cost. The title to the so-called commissioned goods does not pass on to the agent; the things intended for sale remain property of the principal and the things obtained by sale directly become property of the principal upon their passing over to the agent by the third party.

After arranging the matter, the commissionary agent is bound to inform the principal and to submit an account report. The report must contain the name of the person with whom the commissionary agent concluded the contract with the consequences given in the Civil Code.

The commissionary agent is bound, after procuring the matter, to transfer the rights and things obtained in arranging the matter on the principal, and the principal is bound to take them.

Even though the contract with the commissionary agent is basically a contract for payment, an agreement on the particular payment is not an essential term of the contract. If payment has not been agreed on, the commissionary agent is entitled to a usual payment, that is, at the amount usual at the time of conclusion of the contract. Along with the payment, the principal is bound to reimburse the necessary or useful costs incurred to the agent while performing his/her obligation.

To withdrawal from the contract by the commissionary agent or the principal, stipulations under the Civil Code apply and are similar to those for withdrawal of mandatary or mandator in relation to contract of mandate. The principal is entitled to withdraw the mandate only until the broker is committed to a third party.

§4. Forwarding/Shipping Agency

132. With a forwarding contract the shipper undertakes, at his/her costs, to procure the shipping of goods for the principal from a particular place to another place and to procure or carry out other acts relating to the shipping, and the principal undertakes remunerate him for that. If remuneration has not been agreed upon, the shipper is entitled to usual remuneration; in addition, he is entitled to remuneration of purposefully expended costs.

Potential agreed acts consisting in collecting acts of the shipper before delivering the goods or before issuing a respective document on how the goods are to be handled are adequately governed by provisions on documentary collection.

If the contract has not been concluded in writing, the shipper is entitled to demand delivery of the shipping order from the principal.

The shipper is obliged to make insurance for the goods only if it has been agreed upon.

The shipper may engage another shipper (intermediate shipper).

The principal may, in or outside the contract, ban the carrying out of the transport by the shipper himself/herself.

The receiver of the goods is liable by taking possession of the goods for the claim of the shipper from the contract towards the principal if he/she knew or must have known about it. For the time of detention of the goods or the documents on how to handle the goods, the shipper has a security interest in the goods for securing the principal's debts resulting from the contract. In other issues, the shipping is governed adequately by rules on commission.

§5. Commercial Agency

133. With a commercial agency contract, the agent as an independent business person is obliged to involve himself/herself, over the long term, for the benefit of the party represented in an activity directed to conclusion of a certain type of contract (businesses), or to bargain and agree on businesses on behalf of the party represented and at his/her cost.

The contract must be concluded in writing.

The stipulations of commercial agency that will not apply include:

- the agents whose activities are not paid;
- persons involved in securities exchange or commodities exchange.

Contrary to the agency contract, which relates to conclusion of a single specified contract, what is typical of a commercial agency contract is continuity of the commercial agent's activities creating a permanent relationship between the commercial agent and the party represented; however, it is not an employment relationship. This activity may concern contract of sale, contract for work or other contracts – but always those contracts involving a certain type of goods or activities, and not all contracts that may be concluded by the particular represented business person.

The subject matter of the agent's obligation is searching for the persons interested in doing business as specified in the contract. Thus, this activity is of a factitious nature, and therefore no legal relationship arises between the agent and the person represented without any other steps taken because it is so in the contract of mandate between the mandatary and the mandator. If the contract expressly stipulates that the business agent is authorized to carry out juridical acts on behalf of the person represented, that is, to do business in his/her name, the respective rights and duties are governed by the respective stipulations on the contract of mandate. Without being granted procuration, the business agent is not authorized to do business on behalf of the person represented, receive anything for him/her, or carry out other juridical acts. If the contract also includes an authorization to do business on behalf of the person represented, the business agent is bound to carry out these business functions only according to the terms stated by the person represented, unless the person represented has expressed his/her consent to another manner of acting.

The commercial agent is bound to carry out the activity he/she has been obliged to do honestly, with reasonable care and bona fide; he/she is bound to take care of the interests of the party represented, according to authorizing and reasonable instructions of the party represented and to give the party represented the necessary information available. He/she also informs the party represented on the development in the market and all circumstances important for the interests of the party represented, mainly those related to decision-making in doing business. If the business agent cannot carry out his/her activities, he/she must inform the party represented without unnecessary delay.

In relation to the commercial agent, the party represented is bound to act honestly and bona fide; he/she is bound mainly:

- to provide the agent with the necessary documents related to the subject matter of business; the documents are in ownership of the represented person and he/she will return them after the end of the representation;
- to provide the information necessary to perform the obligations arising from the commercial agency contract, within a reasonable time to inform the business agent that he/she presumes a significant reduction of activities as compared to what the agent could reasonably expect.

The party represented is also bound to inform the commercial representative within a reasonable time that he/she has accepted, refused or failed to perform the act provided for by the agent.

The commercial agent may neither inform other persons on the data obtained within agency without the consent of the party represented, nor use it for himself/herself or for other persons, if it is contrary to the interests of the party represented. This duty pertains even after termination of the commercial agency contract.

The business agent guarantees fulfilment of the obligations by the third party to whom the agent proposed the party represented do business with, or in the name of whom he/she has done business on behalf of the party represented, only if he/she was obliged to do so in writing and if he/she has obtained a premium for taking over the liability. His/her rights and obligations are further governed by the stipulations on liability assumption.

The commercial agent is entitled to a commission, the amount of which is, as a rule, stipulated in the contract. If not, the commercial agent is entitled to the commission as common in the trade usage in relation to the place of his/her activities and with regard to the type of goods involved in the commercial agency contract. If there is no such usage, the agent will be entitled to reasonable remuneration, considering all aspects of the acts carried out. Every part of the remuneration, which varies according to the amount and value of the business, is deemed a part of the commission. In addition to the commission, the agent is entitled to claim the costs incurred in his/ her activities, only if so stipulated and if nothing contrary arises from the contract and when a right to the commission arose to him/her from the businesses related to the costs. The right to commission and cost reimbursement does not arise when the agent acted in the business as a commercial agent or broker for the person with whom the party represented has concluded a contract of the business involved.

Under the conditions stipulated in sections 2514–2517, the commercial agent is entitled to special remuneration after termination of the representation.

If a decisive territory has not been agreed upon, then it is the territory of the Czech Republic; in the case of a foreign agent, it is the territory of the State where the business agent has his/her seat at the time of the conclusion of the contract.

Some rights and obligations of the parties to the business agency contract differ according to whether they are *non-exclusive or exclusive commercial agencies.*

If exclusive agency is involved, the party represented is bound to employ no other business agent within the territory stated and for the range of businesses stipulated. The business agent is not authorized to carry out, in this extent, business agency for other persons or to do business at his/her own cost or another person's cost. Breach of this duty establishes liability for damages – even though not stipulated under the contract – and both the commercial agent and the represented party are by law entitled, depending on the circumstances, to withdraw from the contract. In exclusive commercial agency, the party represented is entitled to do other business related to this exclusive agency even without the commercial agent's cooperation, but the party is bound – unless stipulated otherwise in the contract – to pay commission from this business to the agent as if the business were done in cooperation with the agent.

Contrary to exclusive commercial representation, in non-exclusive representation the party represented may also authorize other persons to carry out business agency for him/her, which was agreed on with the commercial agent, and the commercial agent may carry out activities he/she obliged to towards the party represented, at his/her own cost or at another person's cost.

The commercial agent obligation terminates upon the term for which the contract was concluded.

In the commercial agency contract, it may be agreed in writing that the commercial agent may not, for a time specified, but no longer than two years after termination of the contract, carry out an activity that was the subject matter of the commercial agency, or another activity that would be competitive for the business of the party represented, at his/her own cost or at another person's cost. A competition clause contrary to these terms will be invalid. In case of doubt, the court may restrict or declare invalid a competitive clause that would restrict the agent more than necessary for the inevitable protection of the party represented.

Chapter 11. Bailment (Contract on Custody, Deposit)

§1. Bailment

134. Under Czech Civil Code, bailment is a legal relationship in which the bailee is bound to take over a thing from the bailor for bailment and to take care of it properly. Legal relationship arises from an agreement on bailment, which should contain the clauses on the thing being taken over, on remuneration as a rule and on the period of the bailment. There is no written form prescribed for bailment. However, it is possible to hand over and to take over the thing by using technical means.

135. The bailor:

- is entitled to hand over the thing to the bailee to hold it on trust; the custody must be carried out in the manner agreed, or diligently, if the manner of bailment was not agreed upon;
- is entitled to demand returning the thing at any time unless agreed or evident from the circumstances for how long the thing should be in bailment;
- is obliged to compensate the loss arising from bailment to the bailee as well as the costs incurred to the bailee in carrying out his/her duty.

The bailee:

- is entitled to hand over the thing in bailment to another bailee if this option was agreed in the contract;
- is entitled to reimbursement of the necessary costs incurred during the custody of the thing;
- is entitled to a remuneration if agreed, or if the remuneration is consistent with the business of the bailee, or if it is common in contact between the parties;
- is obliged to return the thing to the bailor when required, even before lapse of the period of the bailment agreed;
- has the right to return the thing any time unless the period of bailment is agreed on or is evident from the circumstances.

Both the bailor and the bailee may claim their mutual rights arising from the bailment during a period of no more than three months. If the right is claimed belatedly, the court will not recognize the protest of the other party.

Special instances of liability are stipulated as follows:

(a) if the bailee uses the thing bailed or allows another person to use it, or hands it over to another person for bailment without the bailor's consent or unless necessary, or if he/she is delayed in returning it, he/she is liable for even incidental damage arising – unless the damage would have affected the thing in bailment anyway;
(b) the bailor is liable for the damage arising to the bailee through bailment as well as for the costs incurred to the bailee in carrying out his/her duty.

Unless there are general grounds for termination of the contract, the following may be applied:

- lapse of time for which the bailment was agreed (if agreed); – performing the right to demand returning the thing by the bailor even before lapse of the agreed period;
- performing the right to demand returning the thing by the bailor or returning the thing by the bailee, unless the period for bailment has been agreed on or is evident from the circumstances.

§2. Custody of Securities

136. The custodian keeps the securities in custody separately from his/her securities or the securities of other custodians unless agreed otherwise or unless it is a collective custody. The custodian keeps record of the securities deposited in his/her custody. In collective custody, the securities are kept together with the securities of other custodians separately from the custodian's securities. The share of each of the custodians is determined by the ratio of the sum of the nominal values of his/her deposited securities and the sum of all the securities in collective custody. The securities in custody may be put into another custodian's custody (secondary custody).

Immobilization of securities occurs when the issuer of securities puts these securities into collective deposit; a security is issued on the day when the issuer gave it to the custodian on behalf of its owner as the first acquirer. The name of the owner is not mentioned in putting the security in custody, in securities to name and securities to order. The owner of the deposited security has the right to demand his deposited security to be given to him/her only under the conditions set in the conditions of securities issue. The custodian of the immobilized securities may only be a person authorized to keep a separate record of investment instruments under a special law. A secondary custodian may only be the person authorized to keep records following the separate record of investment instruments under a special law.

§3. Storage

137. Fundamental provisions stipulate that the storage keeper obliges himself/herself under the contract of storage to take over a thing in order to store it and take care of it, and the ordering party obliges himself/herself to pay the storage charges. If storage is the storage keeper's object of business activity, the refutable presumption applies that the parties have concluded contract of storage.

Based on the fundamental provision, the essential terms of the contract are as follows:

- parties to the contract denoted: the storage keeper and the ordering party;
- object of storage denoted: the thing stored, which may be, unlike under contract of bailment, given to be stored only after the contract was concluded;

– agreement on payment: storage charges; – the obligation of the storage keeper to take over, store, and take care of the thing.

Comparing fundamental provisions of contract of bailment and contract of storage, it arises that if taking care of a thing is not the subject matter of business of the keeper, it applies that the parties have concluded a contract of bailment. Provisions of the contract of storage stipulate that if care of thing is subject matter of business of the keeper, the parties have concluded a contract of storage. This criterion – the subject matter of business – may distinguish the type of the contract concluded. An essential term of the contract is denoting the subject matter of storage by the storage keeper and the ordering party. Unlike the contract of bailment, when the thing is given no later than upon conclusion of the contract (it is the thing that the bailee has with him/her), under the contract of storage, the thing can be handed over only after conclusion of the contract.

A storage contract need not have a written form; however, it is stipulated that the storage keeper is bound to confirm the goods takeover in writing. A certificate of taking possession of a thing may be substituted with a warehouse receipt which is a security (*see* more in sections 2417–2418 C.C.). The contract may be concluded for a fixed term of indefinite duration. If the time is not stipulated in the contract, a refutable presumption applies that the contract is concluded for an indefinite period. In such a case, the ordering party may demand release of the thing at any time, and the contract will be discharged upon its return; the storage charges relate only to the real time of storage. If the storage was agreed for a fixed period of time, the ordering party may take over the thing prior to the lapse of the period agreed, but in such a case, the storage keeper is entitled to storage charges for the whole period of storage agreed on. If the ordering party has taken over the thing before the lapse of the time agreed, he/she may take use of the term agreed and have the thing stored again, of course, paying to the storage keeper the respective costs.

Liability for delay may arise in relation to taking or giving the thing and the storage charges payment.

The obligation arising from the contract becomes extinct, in addition to general ground, usually by:

(a) lapse of time stated to the ordering party for giving the thing to the storage keeper (unless agreed otherwise, if the ordering party has not given the thing within six months after making the contract);
(b) releasing the thing stored to the ordering party upon the contract for an indefinite term;
(c) lapse of time agreed for storage;
(d) a one-month notice by the storage keeper (Unless agreed otherwise, the storage keeper is entitled to repudiate the contract after a one-month notice. The term starts running on the first day of the month following the month in which the notice has been served on the ordering party. The fact that the notice term is bound to its serving must be taken into consideration when giving it.);
(e) The discharge of the contract without time of notice by the storage keeper:
   – if the ordering party has not disclosed a dangerous nature of the thing, and there is serious risk of damage to the storage keeper;

- if the ordering party owes storage charges for at least a three-month term;
- if there is a risk of substantial damage to the thing stored, which cannot be prevented by the storage keeper.

After the discharge of the contract, the storage keeper may state a reasonable period of time for taking over the thing with a warning that he/she would sell the thing otherwise. After lapse of this period, the storage keeper may sell the thing in a suitable way at the cost of the ordering party. The storage keeper may deduce storage charges as well as the costs incurred in relation to the sale from the proceeds and must pay the rest to ordering party without an unnecessary delay.

Chapter 12. Transportation

§1. Transportation of Persons and Things

138. Obligations during transportation secure the needs arising in relation to transportation of natural persons in vehicles, their luggage, as well as carriage of goods. A transportation relationship arises between the carrier (the business person carrying out transportation) and the traveller, the sender and the recipient. The basic distinction of transportation relationships is transportation of persons (transportation of passengers and their luggage) and carriage of goods.

I. Transportation of Persons (Passengers)

139. Transportation of passengers is a service provided to passengers involved in transporting and shipment of the items (travellers and their luggage, including the instances when each is transported separately) by a means of transport to their destination, properly and on time, for a fare stated.

Distinguishing the manner, how a luggage is transported (i.e., together with the passenger and under his/her supervision or separately from the passenger) is decisive for liability for the damage caused to a thing.

For transportation of persons, it is also significant whether it is a regular or irregular transportation and whether it is carried out either individually or in groups.

Legal relationship in transportation of persons arises by a contract between the passenger who may be any natural person capable of satisfying the terms stated by rules of transport and fares, and the carrier.

Legal regulation of transportation of persons is included in the Civil Code. More detailed rules are given by special regulations, usually rules of transportation and fares (these regulation become part of the contract for transportation if accepted by the contractual parties). Rules of transportation may, under this regulation, include stipulations effective in international transportation for the inland transport; liability for damages to health as stated by the Civil Code may not be restricted.

Rights and obligations of a passenger:

- duty to pay the fare for the transportation as stated; the amount of the fare is determined by transportation rules or tariffs that also stipulate the instances when the passenger is entitled to transportation free of charge, or to a reduced price;
- duty to pay the price for luggage transportation;
- duty to observe relevant stipulation of the rules of transport and fares for the particular way of transportation and to observe the carrier's instructions (cf. rules of transportation).

Rights and obligations of a carrier:

- duty of care especially for safety and comfort of passenger during transportation and in group public transportation to enable them to use social and cultural facilities;

- the duty of care for the luggage (transported separately) to be transported to its destination no later than simultaneously with the passenger;
- the right to sell uncollected items transported under similar conditions as in failure to collect repaired or adjusted things.

Liability for delay under the Civil Code is outlined only when relevant stipulations are contained in the rules of transportation. This applies mainly to regular public transport. In irregular transport, the carrier is liable for delayed transport only if the passengers have suffered damage as a result. The terms and extent of compensation are stipulated under the rules of transportation, too. A claim arising from liability must be claimed against the carrier without delay, no later than within six months. The respective rights the court will not recognize protests of the other party if not claimed within this period.

The carrier is liable for damage caused to health or luggage transported together with the passenger, or to the things he/she had on him/her, under the stipulations on liability for damage caused during the operation of the means of transport. The liability of the carrier for damage occurred during the transportation of the luggage transported separately from the passenger is stipulated under provisions on liability for carriage of goods.

The legal relationship terminates as generally applicable (usually by performance); the Civil Code contains no specific provisions.

II. Carriage of Goods

140. Carriage of goods is a transportation provided to the consigner involving transportation of a consignment to its destination and then handing it over to the consignee. A legal relationship arises between the consigner and the carrier by contract for which no specific form is prescribed. The consigner is bound to confirm the order to the carrier in writing if and when required, and the carrier is obliged to confirm taking over the consignment to the consigner in writing if and when required. The article may be any movable thing if consistent with the terms of transportation rules, that is, capable to be transported. The parties of the legal relationship are predominantly the carrier and the consigner, but it may also be the consignee, unless the consignor and the consignee are the same person.

Legal regulation for carriage of goods is included in the Civil Code. More detailed regulation of carriage of goods is given in special rules, usually rules for transportation and rates (these rules become part of the contract for carriage if accepted by the parties to the contract). Here, the rules for transportation in inland transportation may take over stipulations applicable in international transportation.

Rights and obligations:

(a) of the consigner:
- duty to pay the rate for carriage of the consignment;
- duty to confirm the order of consignment if required;
- right to issue new instruction consistent with the terms stated by rules of consignment.

(b) of the consignee:
- the duty to take over the consignment in its destination; unless done so within six months, the carrier is entitled to sell the item (rules of transport may state the terms for taking over certain items within a time shorter than six months);
- right to give new instructions to the carrier is granted by the transportation rules and consistent with the terms stated under them.

(c) of the carrier:
- the duty to transport the carriage of consignment to its destination;
- the duty to confirm in writing the taking over of the consignment if required; a certificate may be substituted with a bill of loading (*see* more in sections 2572–2577 C.C.);
- the duty to carry out the carriage expertly and within the term stated;
- the duty to hand over the consignment in its destination to the intended consignee;
- right to also employ other transporters in transporting the carriage involved;
- right to sell uncollected consignments under the terms similar to those applicable for uncollected repaired of adjusted things.

Liability for damage arising on the consignment transported at the time between taking it over and handing it over, regardless of faultiness, is specifically stipulated under the Civil Code. The reasons for leeway result from the situation when the carrier is not liable for the damage caused by the consigner or the consignee; for faulty article, packaging, or cover; or for the special nature of the consignment or a circumstance that could not be averted by the carrier. The respective reasons may be itemized in rules of transportation. In case of loss or consignment destroying the carrier, he/she is obliged to compensate the price that the lost or destroyed consignment had at the time of being taken over to be transported. The carrier is further obliged to bear necessary costs incurred in relation with the lost or destroyed article. Compensation is preferred, unless repair of the thing is reasonable, in which case the cost is borne by the carrier. The carrier is also liable for damages arising from exceeding the delivery term; the terms and remedies are stated by the transportation rules. The carrier is always the liable person, even in cases when other persons transport the carriage. When the transportation is carried out jointly by several carriers as a joint transportation, the transportation rules state which carrier will be liable for this transport – and under what terms.

Recovery for damage must be claimed against the carrier within six months after the consignment has been handed over to the consignee, or, if the consignment was not handed over at all, within six months after taking over the consignment to be transported. Rights not claimed in fixed terms are not recognized by the court if protested by the other party.

Discharge of obligations arises under general terms, by performance as a rule. Transportation rules may stipulate some specific ways of discharge.

§2. Operating a Means of Transportation

141. A fundamental provision of this contract type establishes that, under the contract for operation of a means of transport, the operator obliges himself/herself to transport a shipment denoted by the party ordering and to carry out one or more trips denoted in advance using the means of transport in question, or, during the term agreed, to carry out trips as denoted by the ordering party when the ordering party obliges himself/herself to pay the charges. Contrary to the contract for operation of a means of transport, in case of lease contract for a means of transport, there is only a lease without providing the personnel, fuel, and an obligation to carry out one or more trips. Fundamental terms of the contract are:

- parties to the contract denoted: operator of the means of transport and the party ordering the operation of a means of transport;
- the obligation of operator to transport a shipment;
- denoting the means of transport;
- denoting the trip to be carried out by the means of transport, or the time, during which the means of transport is to transport the consignment;
- obligation of the ordering party to pay for the transport.

The ordering party may assign the right from the contract to another person.

If the transporting party takes over a load for transportation, the provisions on the contract of transportation are adequately applied for determining rights and duties of the parties if the nature of the contract on transportation allows that.

Chapter 13. Obligations from Contract of Account, One-Time Deposit, Letter of Credit, and Collection

§1. Account

142. By an account the bank obliges itself to set up, since the time stated and for the currency stated, a current account for its owner. By creating a current account, a business contract relationship arises between the bank and the account owner, in which the account serves as a form of accounting for mutual debts and obligations between them. The bank is bound to receive and to record within the assets the money deposits or payment made for the benefit of the account owner, and according to the owner's instructions, it carries out payments and withdrawals of money from the owner's account.

Fundamental terms of the contract are bargaining the bank's obligation to open a current account for the owner, stating the time since it has been set up, and outlining the currency of the account. The contract may be repudiated by the owner at any time. The account can be set up for one or more owners, all having the position of the account owner and all dealing with the account together.

If the parties have agreed to draw more financial means from the account than it includes the provisions on credit are applied.

The payment account is regulated by a special law. A special law also regulates transfer of money at another than payment account if this transaction is regulated by another law.

An account other than the payment one is regulated in sections 2670–2675. These also regulate the depositing of cash to the payment account and transfer of financial means at the payment account if it is not a transaction pursuant to another law.

With the savings book, the issuer confirms depositing the cash and drawing it from the account. Such an account does not serve the purpose of transferring money. The savings book may only be issued at the name of its owner.

§2. One-Time Deposit

143. The contract of one-time deposit means an obligation of the depositor to provide the recipient of the deposit with a one-time deposit at a certain amount and the deposit recipient undertakes to accept it and, after the termination of the obligation, to return it and to pay the depositor an interest (*see* more in section 2680).

§3. Letter of Credit

144. With the letter of credit contract, the drawer undertakes to the principal to draw, at his/her request and at his/her account, a letter of credit for the benefit of a third person and the principal undertakes to pay the drawer remuneration. The obligation arises by drawing the letter of credit. The drawer will inform the beneficiary in writing that he/she is drawing a letter of credit for his/her benefit and will inform him/her about its content. The letter of credit includes at least:

- an obligation of the drawer to pay a certain amount of money, to accept a bill of exchange or another performance;
- the letter of credit terms with determining the time of their fulfilment by the beneficiary so that he/she could demand performance from the drawer.

The drawer will provide the beneficiary from the letter of credit with performance under the conditions set in the letter of credit.

The letter of credit may be, at the request of the drawer, confirmed by another drawer, which gives the beneficiary right to demand performance from the confirming drawer, too.

The letter of credit obliges the drawer to provide the beneficiary with performance if the documents determined by the letter of credit are submitted in time. With other letters of credit, provisions on the documentary letter of credit are applied (*see* more in sections 2687–2693).

§4. Collection

145. The purpose of the contract of collection is the obligation of the procurer of collection to procure for the principal acceptance of an amount of money or another collecting act from a third person, and the principal's obligation to pay remuneration to the procurer of collection. If remuneration has not been agreed upon, the principal will pay the procurer of collection such remuneration that is usual at the time of the conclusion of the contract.

The procurer of collection will call upon the third person to perform a collecting act. If the third person refuses to do it, the procurer will inform the principal about it without unnecessary delay. If the procurer proceeds with professional care and according to the principal's instructions and despite that he/she does not perform the collection, no sanction may be applied against the procurer.

The subject matter of the collection is handed over by the procurer to the principal without unnecessary delay. A special variant is the documentary letter of credit on the basis of which the procurer will give the third person documents after having been paid a certain amount of money or after another collecting act has been performed and the principal undertakes to pay remuneration to the procurer of the collection.

Chapter 14. Aleatory Obligations

146. The Civil Code regulates the category of obligations from the so-called aleatory contracts which are characterized by their depending on profit or non-profit from an uncertain event for at least one of the contractual parties (section 2756).

§1. Insurance

147. The Civil Code included in the fourth part of Chapter II (sections 2758–2872) a legal regulation of insurance so far regulated in the special Act No. 37/2004 Col. on Insurance Contract. It meant a unification of the previous two-line character of the legal retime of insurance relationships since the relationships originated until 31 December 2001 were still regulated by the provision of the Civil Code No. 40/1964 and the legal relationships originated since 1 January 2005 were regulated by a special law.

The insurance arises on the basis of an insurance contract with which the insurer undertakes to the policyholder to provide him/her or a third person with a payment if an insurance event occurs (i.e., accidental event covered by the insurance) and the policyholder undertakes to pay the insurer an insurance premium. The insurance contract has to be concluded always in writing unless the insurance has been agreed upon for a period shorter than one year, or if the policyholder accepted the offer by paying the insurance premium in time. The insurance contract is considered to be a kind of contract for financial service (section 1841) which is regulated by special provisions on consumer protection (section 1810 and subsequent ones) and if a means of distance communication has exclusively been used for concluding the contract.

Achieving the purpose of insurance is ensured by the definition of insurance interest as a justified need of protection against an insurance event (section 2761), which is supposed to prevent speculative types insurance (e.g., wager policy). The policyholder has an insurance interest in his/her own life and health, or life and health of a third person as well as in his/her own property (in this case, a future insurance interest may be insured, too); if the interested person did not have an insurance interest and the insurer knew or must have known about that when concluding the contract then the contract is invalid; when the insurance interest is terminated then the insurance is terminated, too. The subject matter of the insurance may also be a foreign insurance danger.

The insurance arises on the first day after making the insurance contract unless it is agreed that it will arise by the conclusion of the contract or later. It may also exceptionally be agreed that the insurance covers the period before the conclusion of the insurance contract.

The subject matter of the insurance relationship may be determined by reference to the insurance terms which usually detail the origin, duration and termination of the insurance, the insurance event, the exclusion from insurance and the manner of determining the extent of the insurance performance and its maturity; the insurer is obliged to inform the policyholder about them before concluding the contract.

The insurer will issue to the policyholder a policy as a receipt evidencing the conclusion of the insurance contract. If the policy is lost, damaged or destroyed, the insurer will issue a copy of the policy at the request and costs of the policyholder. If the insurance contract stipulates the duty to submit the policy in order to assert the right to premium, the insurer may demand paying off the original policy before issuing a copy of it.

The insurance contract may also be made for the benefit of a third person; it means that the insurance contract is made by the policyholder with the insurer for the benefit of the insured. For such a contract, general provisions of the Civil Code about contract for the benefit of a third person will be used, and the consent of the third person may be given additionally after asserting the right to the premium.

The third person has a right to the insurance performance if the insured person, or his/her legal representative, has given the third person consent to accept the insurance performance after being made acquainted with the content of the contract. In certain specified cases, the law may impose on a certain person the duty to make an insurance contract – the so-called compulsory insurance (e.g., the compulsory motor vehicle liability insurance, various types of professional insurance – for advocates, notaries, etc.).

Rights and duties arise for the parties by concluding the contract. Since the day of the conclusion of the contract (or the day agreed in the insurance contract) the insurer's right to premium arises. Maturity depends on agreement but the ordinary premium is payable since the first day of the period of cover and the lump sum premium since the day when the period of cover starts to run. The insurer has principally right to premium for the duration of cover. If an insurable event happens in consequence of which a private insurance is terminated, the insurer has the right to the premium till the end of the period of cover during which the event happened; as for the lump sum premium the insurer is entitled to it for the whole period for which the private insurance was agreed (unless provided otherwise in law or agreed otherwise). The insurance contract may stipulate terms under which the insurer is entitled, in connection with changes of terms decisive for establishing the amount of premium except for changes of age and health condition of the insured persons, to modify the amount of the ordinary premium for the next period of cover.

The policyholder and the insured have a duty to answer truthfully and completely all written questions of the insurer concerning the insurance. The insurer has the same duty towards the policyholder and the insured. The policyholder has a duty to notify the insurer without any delay that the insurable event happened, to explain truthfully the origin and the consequences of that event, to submit all necessary documents and to proceed in the way agreed in the insurance contract. If the policyholder is not the insured himself/herself, it is the insured that has the above-mentioned duty; if the insurable event is the death of the insured, it is the authorized person that has the duty. The policyholder has the duty to notify the insurer without any delay about a change or the termination of the insurable risk with which the mechanism of proportional modification of the premium or the termination of the insurance relationship corresponds. The insurer has a duty, after notification of the event with which the claim for performance from the insurance is connected, to start without any delay an examination needed for determining the extent of his/her duty to perform. The insurance premium is payable within fifteen days after finishing the examination, which is the moment when the insurer communicates the results to the authorized person (the period for finishing the examination is limited to three months after the notification, at the same time its extension and stopping is regulated). As a consequence of the breach of the duty by the policyholder or the insured, the insurance performance may be proportionally decreased.

Types of Insurance

148. The Civil Code distinguishes two basic forms of insurance:

(1) damage insurance: the purpose of damage insurance is compensation of a damage arisen as a consequence of an insurable event;
(2) sum insurance: the purpose of sum insurance is to gain a sum, that is, an agreed sum of money as a consequence of an insurable event the amount of which does depend on the arising of or the extent of the damage.

According to the subject of insurance, there are traditional types as follows:

(a) insurance of persons;
(b) insurance of assets.

(a) As for insurance of persons, it is possible to insure a natural person for the case of death, for reaching a certain age or for reaching the day set in the insurance contract as the end of insurance, and for the case of injury, illness or another state of affairs linked with health or a change of the personal position of the insured. Within insurance of persons, the following types are distinguished (all of them may be agreed as damage insurance or sum insurance):
   - life insurance (especially for the case of death, for reaching a certain age, for reaching the day determined in the contract as the end of the insurance done or for another state of affairs linked with a change of personal position);
   - injury insurance (for the case of injury, that is, an unexpected and immediate impact of outer forces or one's own personal force regardless of the will of the insured which causes impairment of health or death);
   - insurance for the case of illness or another state of affairs linked with health condition.
(b) Insurance of assets includes insurance of a thing, a set of things or other assets. It holds that insurance of a thing or a set of things may only be made as damage insurance; insurance of other assets may be made as either damage insurance or sum insurance. Within insurance of assets, particular types are distinguished (they may only be made as damage insurance):
   - insurance of legal protection;
   - insurance of liability;
   - insurance of credit and guarantee;
   - insurance of financial losses.

Differences among them are derived from peculiarities of the subject of insurance – insurance of legal protection consists in the undertaking of the insurer to reimburse on the basis of an insurance contract the costs incurred by the insured when enforcing his/her rights to the extent defined in the insurance contract and to provide services directly linked with this private insurance; insurance of liability for damage or another injury is made for the case of the insured being liable for causing damage to another person, the insured having the right to have the damage for which he/she is liable to be paid for by the insurer up to the limit of the agreed premium or at the amount of the damage arisen; insurance of credit includes protection against property consequences that may arise for the insured due to his/her debtor's failing to pay off the provided money; insurance of guarantee is made for the case of performance from a guarantee obligation, forfeiture of bail or security or performance from them (or performance from another similar reason); insurance of financial losses is made for costs incurred due to a harmful event or lost profit or any financial loss.

The right to performance from insurance is statute-barred after three years at the latest, and in the case of life insurance it is ten years (the general option of an agreement to shorten or lengthen the period of limitation is excluded). The right to insurance payment from liability is statute-barred at the latest when the right to compensation of damage or injury which it covers is statute-barred. The limitation period of the right to insurance performance begins to run after one year following the arising of the insurable event. This also holds when direct entitlement to insurance performance has arisen for the aggrieved party against the insurer, or when the insured asks the insurer to pay him/her the amount he/she has given to the aggrieved party as a compensation for the damage for which he/she is liable towards the aggrieved party when fulfilling the duty to compensate damage or another injury.

Termination of insurance occurs at the moment of the termination of the insurance relationship which takes place especially:

- by expiry of the period of cover (unless the mechanism of extension of the period of cover has not been applied);
- as a consequence of the lapse of the period established by the insurer for giving a demand note to pay the premium or its part;
- by an agreement between the insurer and the policyholder;
- by notice of termination from the part of the insurer or the policyholder;
- by withdrawal of the insurer or withdrawal of the policyholder from the contract concluded by the form of distant deal;
- by refusal of performance by the insurer.

There are also the general reasons of the termination of insurance: by termination of insurance risk, by termination of existence of the ensured thing (or another property value), by the death of the insured natural person or by dissolution of the insured legal entity without a legal successor.

§2. Wagering (Betting), Gaming and Drawing a Lot

149. Wagering may be one-sided or two-sided. A one-sided bet is a contract in which one of the parties promises performance to the other party in the case that out of the opposite assertions of the parties the assertion of the party promising proves false. A double-sided bet is a contract in which both parties promise one another the performance for the case that their respective assertions will prove false. Thus, the essentials of wagering (wagering contract) are opposite assertions of the parties on whether a certain fact has existed, does exist or will occur. The respective questionability must be based on lack of knowledge concerning this fact by the parties.

Gaming may be both one-sided or two-sided. In a one-sided gaming, one party promises the other performance dependent on the result of a game which is played according to certain rules. It is basically the same for the two-sided gaming, except that more than one party will actively take part in the game. Unlike wagering, gaming presumes certain activity of the parties (physical or mental, typically, a sport). Gaming will be valid under the condition that the rules stated or agreed upon have been observed.

Criminal law imposes sanctions for running monetary or another similar type of gaming or wagering the rules of which do not guarantee equal opportunities of winning for all the participants.

A lot – as well as a letter in which a performance is promised in the case of a number brought by the lot will be drawn according to certain rules – is considered in a similar manner as wagering or gaming. Common are nowadays also lots where winning is secured in another way, for example, wipe-off lots.

The Civil Code deems the claims to winnings in wagering and gaming as natural obligations, except in the case of an enterprise run by the State or permitted by authorities. Similarly, winnings from bets, games and debts from loans provided knowingly for wagering or gaming cannot be claimed. These are the so-called non-actionable debts (natural obligations). These debts cannot be effectively secured, either. Still, these debts are effective and therefore voluntary performance is possible.

The provisions on wager are not used for contracts made at the commodity stock exchange, on the regulated market, in a multilateral business system or among entrepreneurs about an investment instrument pursuant to the Act on Enterprising on the Capital Market.

To gaming similar provisions as those about wager are applied but if the game requires skilfulness or physical exercises of either party only the provision about unenforceability of returning already given win applies, unless the loser is clearly a person with insufficient mental or intellectual abilities.

To drawing a lot, the provisions about wager apply in a similar manner unless a dispute is supposed to be decided by drawing a lot, a thing in joint ownership to be divided or a decision made by ballot.

Chapter 15. Civil Partnership

150. Partnership of persons arising upon a contract concluded according to sections 2716–2746 of the Civil Code differs from interest association of juridical persons as well as from civic association on associating of citizens, as later amended. The partnership contract is a contract under which several persons associate in order to contribute jointly to accomplish economic purpose. This partnership is not a legal entity. Thus, the respective rights do not arise to the partnership as such but to its members.

Essentials of a partnership contract are:

- partnership of persons (without any restrictions as to the number of members; these can be both natural and juridical persons, persons both involved and not involved in business; however, if the partnership has been founded for the purpose of conducting business, its members may only be those authorized to carry out business however, a company may not have only a single member;
- joint contribution (may involve both property contribution and personal activities);
- restricting the purpose as taken out (may be both occasional and permanent).

No special form of contract is prescribed by law. However, if the property is put together, for the validity of the contract the members' deposits list must be signed by them. A rebuttable presumption holds that only the property recorded in the register has been put together.

Each of the participants is bound to develop activities in order to accomplish an economic purpose consistent with the manner stated in the contract and to refrain from any activity that might make accomplishment of this goal impossible or impaired.

According to the nature of contribution (property or work contribution), the members have the following rights and obligations:

The member is obliged to provide property values for the purposes of the partnership by the time stated under the contract, or without any unnecessary delay after conclusion of the contract. The money provided or other things stated in kind are in a joint ownership of all members with respect to the portion of their own contribution. Other things become the members' joint property if they were evaluated with money. The number of joint shares corresponds to the amount of the individual member's deposits.

The property obtained in performing joint activities becomes joint property owned by all members. The shares of this property are equal, unless stated otherwise by contract.

The member may undertake to contribute to the partnership only with his/her activities or only with his/her property. The members are jointly and severally liable to third persons. As a rule, the members decide on arranging common matters by majority vote; in this case, each member has one vote, while the amount of his/her share is not decisive.

An agreement is possible under which disposal of certain things will be delegated to certain members or to a third person. Then the right of each and every member, including those who do not perform administration, must be observed to obtain information on the economy of the partnership.

The members are jointly and severally liable for breach of obligations.

Extinction of partnership occurs mainly by fulfilling its purpose, by lapse of the term for which the partnership was established or the purpose of the partnership becomes impossible. Of course, an agreement of the members to wind up the partnership is also possible. In this instance, the members are entitled to demand the return of the values provided for the partnership activities. Parties settle the property obtained by their common activities within the partnership in the manner stated in the contract. Unless the manner of settlement has been contractually specified, they will settle by equal shares. It is a winding up of a partnership, and it will apply also to other cases of partnership extinction.

Except absolute extinction of partnership, termination of someone's party membership must be considered, that is, termination of membership. This may occur by quitting or excluding, or by death (as well as by extinction of a juridical person).

Basically, any member may quit at any time. However, he/she may not quit at an unsuitable time or at the cost of the other members of the partnership. This restriction does not apply if the reason for quitting is serious; in such case, quitting is possible at any time regardless of whether term of notice has been taken out. In other cases, notice term is to be respected. By quitting the legal relationship of the member in the partnership, the contract is revoked, and he/she must receive back the things brought to the partnership. He/she will be paid the money corresponding to the state of the property share corresponding to the state on the day of his/her quitting.

However, a member may be excluded for serious reasons only detailed in section 2740. After excluding the member, the property settlement must be carried out according to the same principles as in the case of quitting the partnership.

If a partnership member dies and unless the contract contains the respective provisions that his/her heirs take over his/her place, his/her membership in the association should be deemed extinct. In such a case, the heir of a partner has a right to have the membership in the partnership settled. If the partnership contract applies to heirs, too, the heir of the deceased partner enters the partnership instead of the deceased partner.

Chapter 16. Silent Partnership

151. Under a silent partnership contract, a silent partner obliges himself/herself to provide for the businessperson a certain investment and to participate in his/her business activities, and the businessperson obliges himself/herself to pay him/her certain part of the profit – after deducing the obligatory allotment to the reserves fund, if the businessperson is bound to create this fund – corresponding to the investment of the silent partner in the results of the business. In the silent partner contract, the extent of the silent partner's participation in profits and losses must be agreed on equally. Essential terms of the silent partnership contract are stating the investment to be deposited by the silent partner and stating the part of profit related to the silent partner's share as the result of business activities the businessperson obliges himself/herself to pay to the silent partner.

By conclusion of the contract, no legal person – for example, a corporation – is created but an obligation relationship between the silent partner and the given businessperson is established. Any person (a natural person or a legal person), regardless of whether an entrepreneur or not, may be a silent partner. However, the contract party to a silent partner must be a businessperson under section 420 C.C.

As implied in law, a silent partnership contract is always concluded by the businessperson and one silent partner. This does not exclude conclusion of several silent partnership contracts with several different silent partners, among whom no relation similar to the relationship of business partners arises.

The investment of a silent partner may comprise a certain amount of money, a certain thing, a right or other property value usable in business activities. A silent partner is bound to give the subject matter of investment to the businessperson or to enable him/her to utilize it in business at the time agreed or otherwise without an unnecessary delay after conclusion of the contract. Unless stipulated otherwise in the contract, upon taking over the thing, the businessperson becomes its owner; the exception is real property. If real property is the subject matter of investment, the businessperson is entitled to use it for the time of the existence of the contract. If the subject matter of investment is a right and the contract does not stipulate otherwise, the businessperson is entitled to exercise it during the time of the contract existence. Thus, monetary investment and an investment by a thing increase the given businessperson's assets and become part of its business assets. If the investment involves a right to use a thing, then during the time the contract is in effect, the silent partner may not deal with the investment, even though he/she remains its owner.

A silent partner is entitled to have access to business documents and account records related to the business he/she participates in and is entitled to demand a copy of annual balance accounts. Thus, it implies that silent partner does not participate directly in business activities and therefore has no influence on decision taking in business matters. The annual final account is a basis for calculation of the silent partner's share; therefore, he/she has right to demand its copy. The right to the share of the profit, for whose calculation decisive is the final account, arises to the silent partner within thirty days after completing the final account. If the businessperson is a legal entity, the term starts running after approving this final account according to the respective Articles of Association, deed of partnership or law. The silent partner is not bound to return the share received in case of a later loss. The law further stipulates that the silent partner's investment will be reduced by the portion of the loss suffered. In the years to come, the reduced investment will be increased by the profit share, and the right to the share in the profit arises to the partner after attaining the original amount of investment. A silent partner is not bound to provide additional investment in case of loss in business activities, and he takes part in the loss only up to the amount of his/her investment. Therefore, the time during which right to the share in profit arises to the silent partner differs, depending on whether the businessperson given is a natural person or a company. Principally, the right arises upon the final account, and it is an independent right. Therefore, in case of profit share in one year and a loss in the following year, the partner is not bound to return the profit share received. If only losses occurred during the following years, the silent partner is not bound to provide additional investment. The contract terminates if the whole of his/her investment has been exhausted.

Rights and obligations towards third parties in business principally arise to the businessperson. Therefore, it is only the businessperson who acts outwards, and rights and obligations arise to him/her. However, under law a silent partner guarantees for the businessperson's obligations in the two following cases:

(1) if his/her name is contained in the business company of the businessperson;
(2) if he/she announces the person, with whom the businessperson has been bargaining a contract that they are in business together.

If the name of the silent partner stated in the business company of the businessperson were without his/her content, he/she may claim protection in court; in the other cases, it will always be the result of a silent partner's act.

The silent partner's participation terminates in cases stated under the Civil Code. The contract may be concluded both for a fixed or unspecified time. Unless another notice period has been specified in the contract, it may be repudiated no later than six months before the end of the calendar year. Before lapse of the time stated for the silent partnership duration, it is possible, for serious reasons, to demand that the court cancels the obligations arising from the contract. This possibility also applies for a contract concluded for the time not specified. After contract termination (i.e., by extinction of the silent partner's participation by law) or after termination by a court decision, a settlement must be made with the silent partner. The businessperson is bound to return to the silent partner his/her investment, increased or decreased by his/her share in the results of business activities.

Chapter 17. Private Annuity

152. A legal relationship arises between the person entitled and the person owing upon a private annuity contract. This contract provides grounds for the person entitled to be paid a pension for life or for a term of uncertain duration (e.g., during illness or for a temporary period of disability). It is so-called provisory pension supplementing benefits provided from pension insurance. If the duration of an obligation to pension has not been agreed upon, it holds that the duty lasts for the life of the beneficiary.

The person entitled may only be a natural person, which is evident from the nature of the right arisen; the person owing may be both natural and juridical person.

For the pension contract for the lifetime of a person or longer than five years, a written form is prescribed; failure to observe it makes the contract voidable.

A basic right of a pensioner (the person entitled) is the right to payment of the pension benefits as agreed. This right is of personal nature, non-transferable and does not pass on to heirs. However, a claim to a payable benefit may transferred. Benefits may be both monetary and in kind. They are payable in the terms agreed.

With the non-payment pension, the payer may make a reservation for untouchability of the benefits of the receiver in the case of the property seizure or insolvency proceedings but only up to the limit necessary for the receiver's needs.

With the payment pension, it is not possible to withdraw from the contract and claim returning the payment because of not paying the benefits. The court may, in legitimate cases, order the sale of the payer's property for the pension benefits to be paid for an adequate period of time in the future.

The legal relationship becomes extinct first of all by lapse of time for which the contract was taken out, and possibly upon the term of cancellation coming up. The extinction of the legal relationship arises no later than upon the death of the person entitled because it is linked with this person.

Chapter 18. Retired Persons' Housing and Lodging

153. With a contract for retired persons' housing and lodging the owner of a real estate makes a reservation for himself/herself, in connection with its transfer, to have benefits, acts or rights for the purpose of his/her maintenance for the rest of his/her life or for a fixed period, and the acquirer of the real estate undertakes to provide the maintenance. If not agreed and set otherwise, the content of the contract is governed by the local customs. To the contract on retired persons' housing and lodging, the provisions are applied that also regulate rights out of which the housing and lodging consists, especially the easement of the flat or the pension.

If the housing and lodging is established as an easement, the acquirer of the real estate will make all necessary steps needed for recording it in the public register. If the retired person does not waive the right to have the title recorded in the register, it is possible to record the acquirer's title only simultaneously with the recording of the housing and lodging.

The owner of a real estate may record the future housing and lodging in the public register for himself/herself even before the transfer of the real estate.

The person obliged to provide housing and lodging shall assist, even without a special agreement, the retired person who badly needs it due to sickness, injury or in a similar situation. He/she may be released from this duty if he/she manages to place the retired person in a health care or similar institution. If the person obliged to provide housing and lodging is not bound by a special legal reason to pay the costs of the retired person's staying in the institution, the retired person pays the costs by himself/herself.

If the situation has changed and the parties have not agreed the court may, at the motion of the obliged person, decide about the substitution of the provision for housing and lodging with a monetary pension. The court may also, even without a motion, impose on the obliged person the duty to give the operator of a suitable caring institution a certain amount of money as a maintenance security for the benefit of the retired person.

If the provision of housing and lodging has been transformed in a monetary pension, the court may change the agreement of the parties or its own decision if the situation has been substantially changed.

If the building where the retired person's housing was reserved has been destroyed, the obliged person will provide a suitable alternative accommodation at his/her costs.

The housing and lodging for a married couple is not shortened by the death of one of them.

The housing and lodging cannot be assigned; it is only possible to assign the right to payable allowances except for the allowances determined according to personal needs of the retired person.

The right to housing and lodging does not pass to the retired person's heirs.

If a contract for transfer of a real estate has been concluded in connection with establishing housing and lodging, it is not possible to withdraw from it for non-fulfilment of a duty by the person obliged to provide housing and lodging.

Chapter 19. Public Promises

154. A public promise (covenant) is a one-sided juridical act in which it is promised by public declaration that a reward will be paid or other performance will be provided to the persons not defined in case of meeting the terms stated in the promise. Public promise may be made by a natural person or an artificial legal person.

A contractual relationship may arise from a public promise – but not immediately after publishing it. A legal relationship arises only when a person has started executing the performance demanded, or only after meeting the terms stated in the public promise.

In the newly formed legal relationship, the person who announces the promise is bound to grant the reward promised. The Civil Code stipulates, for this instance, that the prize will be granted to the person who is first in fulfilling the public promise terms. The terms may, however, modify the principle so stated.

If several persons have fulfilled the promise terms at the same time, and it follows from the content of the terms that the prize is to be granted to a single person only, the prize will be divided among them equally.

A modification of the public promise is announcing an award for the best performance. For such a promise to be valid, it is necessary to mention the period of time during which one may compete for the award. In other respects, the provision on promising a reward applies. The announcement of an award may be revoked only for serious reasons and it is necessary to compensate the person who has, at least partially, performed the conditions of fulfilling the promise.

Chapter 20. Promise of Compensation

155. With a promise of compensation, the promisor undertakes to compensate the promisee for the damage incurred to him/her from the conduct for which he/she has been asked by the promisor and to which the promisee is not obliged.

The obligation of the promisor arises by the promise being served on the promisee. The promisee is obliged to perform the conduct asked for by the promisor only if he/she has undertaken to do it. The promisor shall compensate the promisee for the costs and all damage incurred to him/her in connection with the conduct asked for. The promisee is obliged to mitigate the extent of damage, though.

Chapter 21. Package Tours (Travel Contract)

156. A legal relationship arises between the travel agent and a traveller on the basis of a travel contract (a special type of the contract for work). Based on this contract, the travel agent obliges himself/herself to provide the traveller with a tour, and the traveller obliges himself/herself to pay the price agreed. The travel agent is the person who offers the tour to the public or to a group of persons in a business manner, which includes offering through a third person. The tour is understood as a combination of at least two of the following items, sold or offered for sale at the overall price, and the service is provided for a period longer than twenty-four hours, or if it includes an accommodation overnight:

- transport;
- accommodation (lodging);
- other services for tourists that do not supplement transport or accommodation and are a significant part of the tour.

The travel agent shall give the customer a certificate of the contract (a certificate of the tour) when the contract is being concluded or immediately after the conclusion. The certificate of the tour must be in writing. If the contract has been made in writing the copy of it will substitute the certificate of the tour if it includes all the elements required for the certificate of the tour.

Together with the certificate of the tour the travel agent shall give the customer a certificate of his/her insurance issued by an insurer pursuant to another legal regulation.

The contracting process has certain specifications because, under the Civil Code, the proposal for travel contract is submitted by the travel agent. The travel contract must contain the essentials prescribed: contractual parties; specification of the tour, mainly the date of its commencing and termination; listing of all services to be provided for the tourists; the price of the tour, including the schedule of payments and the amount of down payment, identification of the manner in which the customer is supposed to assert his/her right for violation of a duty by the travel agent including the information about the period in which he/she may assert his/her right, and at least the amount of compensation which is to be paid by the customer to the travel agent.

The travel agent will also mention in the certificate of the trip if the trip includes:

(a) other services the price of which is not included in the tour price, the information about the number of payments for these services and their amount;
(b) accommodation, information about the location, tourist category, level of comfort, main characteristics and conformity with the legal regulations of the respective country;
(c) transport information about the kind, characteristics and category of the means of transport as well as information about the route of the travel; and
(d) information about boarding, its manner and extent.

If the travel contract fails to contain all these elements, it will be void. Travel contract must also contain further elements, for example, enforcement of claims arising from breach of liability of the travel agent, the amount of settlement, etc. Absence of further elements is sanctioned by the contract being voidable.

The extent of rights and obligations is determined first by fundamental parts of travel contract. Among other rights and obligations, the following may be mentioned:

- the right of the travel agency to increase unilaterally the price of the tour if this option has been agreed on;
- the duty of the travel agency to provide the customer with further detailed information in writing no later than seven days before commencing the tour;
- the right of the travel agency to propose to the customer a change of contractual terms, including the right of the customer to accept the change or to withdraw from the contract;
- the right of the customer to substitute persons;
- the right of the customer to withdraw from the contract;
- the right of the travel agency to withdraw from the contract consistent only with the reasons as stated;
- the duty of the travel agency to pay a fine to the customer in case of the tour cancellation;
- restitution duty of the travel agency and the duty of the customer to pay settlement to the agent after withdrawal from the contract;
- set of obligations concerning securing a substitute performance or removing unfavourable effects caused by the circumstances from outside.

Regarding the breach of rights and obligations of the tour participants (both the customer and the travel agent), usual liability claims arise (liability for delay, liability for damage, liability for defects). They are specified as follows:

- liability of the travel agent for breach of duties, regardless of whether these duties are to be performed by the travel agent himself /herself or by other suppliers of services provided within the tour;
- the term for claiming the rights with the travel agent – both the term of order and preclusion term;
- leeway reasons as stated in favour of the travel agent as well as leeway for general liability for damage;
- limitation of compensation for damage.

The legal relationship becomes extinct in an ordinary manner of termination of contractual relationship, usually by performance.

The Civil Code specifies the termination of legal relationship based on withdrawal from the contract both by the customer (distinguishing the withdrawal consequences and according to the reasons) and on withdrawal by the travel agent (as a consequence of a tour cancellation due to the failure to gain the minimum number of customers or due to breach of duties on the part of the customer).

Chapter 22. Contract for Inspection Activities

157. By the contract for inspection activities, the inspector obliges himself/herself to impartially ascertain the state of a thing or to test results of an activity and to issue a respective evaluation, and the ordering party is bound to pay him/her a fee. There is no written form prescribed for the contract. Fundamental terms of the contract are:

- an obligation to ascertain impartially a state of a thing or to check result of an activity;
- issuing respective attestation;
- payment.

An essential feature of this contract is impartiality because, under a mandatory provision of the Civil Code, the inspector is bound to inspect in an impartial manner and to describe the state ascertained in a respective attestation certificate. The provisions of a contract in question prescribing to the inspector the duties that might influence impartiality of the inspection or correctness of the attestation certificate are deemed invalid by law from the very beginning.

The inspector is bound to exercise reasonable care in the manner stated under the contract, in the extent and manner usual in similar inspections. Further, he/she is bound to carry it out, unless stipulated otherwise in the contract, without an unnecessary delay, in the place where the subject matter of inspection is placed, as given in the contract. Unless the place is determined in the contract, the ordering party is bound to inform the inspector in time about the place and time of the inspection to be carried out.

The right to payment of fee bargained arises to the inspector after complete fulfilment of his/her duties, for example, following an inspection and a respective attestation certificate issued. If the payment has not been agreed upon, the payment will be as usual at the time of conclusion of the contract, with regard to the subject matter, extent, manner and place of inspection. In addition to the bargained, or usual, payment, the ordering party is bound to also pay the inspector the necessary and reasonable costs arisen during inspection, unless they are apparently included in the payment of the fee. If the inspector has evidently not carried out the inspection properly, right to payment of charges and the costs does not arise, and, unless stipulated otherwise under the contract, the ordering party is entitled to withdraw from the contract after the terms stated have lapsed.

Under a cogent provision, carrying out an inspection does not concern legal relationships between the party ordering and other (third) parties, usually between the parties to or from whom the subject matter of inspection comes.

If the inspector breached his/her obligation to carry out the timely inspection and while exercising reasonable care – that is, as proper, and damage arose as a result – he/she is liable for damage. If the subject matter of inspection is quality and quantity of goods, the inspector's liability for compensation of damages is restricted under special regulation as follows: the inspector is bound to compensate damage arisen by breach of duty to carry out the inspection properly only if the damage cannot be made up for by performing the claim of the ordering party in relation to the person liable for the given faulty performance, which is subject to inspection agreed upon between the ordering party and the inspector.

Chapter 23. Quasi-Contracts

§1. Obligations Arising from Unjustified Enrichment

I. General Outline

158. Obligations arising from unjustified enrichment present a special group of obligations that are not due under a contract.

General prerequisites for the unjustified enrichment obligations to arise include mainly the fact that a property benefit – an enrichment – was obtained by the party not entitled. Enrichment may be of various nature (e.g., performance in rem, monetary performance, the benefit of using another person's thing or from performances provided in favour of the enriched person); however, enrichment must always be of a property value with the possibility to be objectively expressed in money. In the property sphere of the person enriched, it will be expressed either in increasing his/her property (direct enrichment) or in the fact that his/her property has not decreased, although in fact it justifiably should have (the so-called indirect enrichment). One person must get enriched at the expense of another, which means that enrichment of one party is simultaneously a detriment of the other one.

The grounds of unjustified enrichment and the corresponding detriments may involve an act of the person enriched (sometimes an illegal act), an act of the aggrieved party, or common conduct of both parties. It may also be an act of a third party or an event. An event may induce unjustified enrichment indirectly, too, if performance of a party to a contract becomes impossible as a result of an event, while the other party has already fulfilled its obligation. Here, obtaining unjustified enrichment is not a direct consequence of an event but the result of the termination of a legal reason (extinction of obligation due to impossibility to perform).

Enrichment must be unjustified. The cases when a certain property benefit can be deemed an unjustified enrichment are expressly stipulated by the Civil Code. It is a demonstrative listing not excluding other reasons. In addition to these special cases, the Civil Code contains a general provision under which 'any person who got enriched without a justified reason at the expense of another must give up the enrichment'.[19]

II. The Obligations Arising from Unjustified Enrichment

159. The Civil Code provides the most frequent facts involving unjustified enrichment. These are cases when a benefit is obtained:

(1) through performance with no legal ground;
(2) through performance upon a terminated legal ground;
(3) unlawful use of someone else's value;

19. See the marg. no. 65. About the prescription of unjustified enrichment see Decision of the Supreme Court from 23.04.2019, 32 Cdo 20/2018/415

(4) through performing by another person what was to be performed by the enriched person:

(a) Unjustified Enrichment Obtained by Performance with No Legal Ground. The unjustified enrichment merits are characterized by the two features:

(i) there was performance – that is, property value was transferred from the property sphere of one party to the property sphere of the other party;

(ii) the performance had no legal ground:

– Performance means a property benefit, presuming that somebody was provided something by it; that is, it must be of such nature that party to which performance was directed obtained a property benefit. The performance may comprise the act of giving something to somebody (a thing, money), passing on a debt and a right established or exercised in favour of somebody (e.g., a work). It may also be a performance involving an omission or a sufferance, but only if the enriched party obtained a property benefit (e.g., a dwelling house owner allows another person to use it).

– Lack of legal grounds for performance may be due to the fact that, from the very beginning, there have been no legal grounds to perform, but the performing party presumed it (performance of no-debt). Further, such cases are included here when an existing debt is performed, but in favour of someone different from the creditor, or by someone different from the debtor, or the performance is of higher value than was due from the obligation. Lack of legal grounds may arise later on, too, but this case is regulated separately. The procedure in case of the lack of a legal ground is also used if the obligation has been cancelled.

(b) Unjustified Enrichment arising from a Terminated Legal Ground. The prerequisites for the right from unjustified enrichment to arise in this case include:

(i) performance provided;

(ii) legal ground for performance provided has terminated:

– This prerequisite comprises similar conclusions as in the case of prerequisites of unjustified enrichment obtained through performance with no legal grounds.

– The grounds for the right to arise include the fact that the legal ground for performance provided has terminated. These are the situations in which, at the time of performance, there existed valid legal grounds, but these legal grounds became ineffective as a result of an incurring subsequent legal event and were thus terminated. It will be so, for example, when a valid withdrawal from a contract occurred for reasons stipulated under law, or under the contract, or when the withdrawal occurred by operation of law when the termination of obligation occurred as a result of the debtor's default in fixed contracts due to impossibility to perform, upon the parties' agreement, or by satisfying a resolutive condition. These also may be the case when performance is provided on the basis of an effective judgment that was subsequently revoked, for example, as a result of a new court trial. However, where a legal ground existed but was terminated prior to performance (e.g., a debt was fulfilled that had become extinct by preclusion; the performance was provided only after the other party effectively has withdrawn from the contract), this will be a performance lacking legal ground, not a performance upon a legal ground later terminated.

- The benefit of unjustified enrichment obtained from performance upon legal grounds that later terminated will be involved only when the legal ground for performance had been valid. The distinction given is of significance, besides others also in the view of expiration of the right to release the unjustified enrichment.

(c) Unjustified Enrichment Obtained from Unfair Sources. An unfair source for obtaining a property benefit can be deemed a manner of obtaining property values that is inconsistent with good morals and, as such, prohibited by law. These are mainly the case when property benefit is obtained through criminal acts, but also the case when certain conduct cannot be criminally sanctioned for some reason (lack of criminal liability as a result of minority or incapacity of the offender).

In an overall assessment of the sources of unfairness, the presumption of fair property benefit applies. Therefore, the party claiming the giving up of property benefit on this ground must prove the source of the unfairness.

(d) Unlawful use of another person's value. It is a newly introduced form of unjustified enrichment requiring the following:
  (i) using another person's value;
  (ii) using must be unlawful (e.g., using another person's vehicle or database without his/her consent).

(e) Unjustified Enrichment Obtained by Another Person's Performance That Was to Be Performed by the Enriched Person. For the obligation to arise, the following prerequisites must be satisfied:
  (i) an existing legal obligation to perform by the party instead of what was performed;
  (ii) performing the legal obligation by the party who was not due to perform:
    - Unjustified enrichment in this case (contrary to the previous case) does not lie in increasing the property of the unjustly enriched person but in the fact that his/her assets got rid of the liabilities as a result of his/her own obligation being performed by another person. Therefore, the legal duty to perform of the owing party is an indispensable prerequisite for the right under the Civil Code. This obligation may be implied in law, in a contract or in another legal situation.

– Another prerequisite is that the party in fact performing has no legal obligation to do so. Therefore, the case when a surety performs to the creditor under the Civil Code is not included here because the surety's duty arises from the surety obligation.

The same principle applied gives the basis for other Civil Code regulations, for example, the landlord's right to demand from the tenant compensation of the costs incurred by small repairs and flat maintenance that were not provided by the tenant himself/ herself and thus carried out by the tenant on his/her cost. In this case, as well as in others, when some rights are specifically stipulated, the special regulation applies that is of significance, usually in the view of the prerequisites to arise.

The person who fulfilled a statute-barred, unactionable or invalid debt due to lack of form does not have right to have the performance returned; similarly, the person who has enriched another person knowing that he/she is not obliged to do that has no right to having the performance returned. However, if someone made a performance intentionally so that the other party should commit an unlawful or impossible thing he/she has no right to claim to have it returned. But if a person made a performance for someone intending to commit an unlawful act and did so in order to prevent it then he/she may claim having it returned.

III. Legal Consequences of Unjustified Enrichment

160. A basic legal consequence of unjustified enrichment is a rise of obligation to release this enrichment. The law specifically stipulates settlement of an invalid or cancelled contract between the parties by expressing a synallagmatic nature of this obligation relationship arisen from unjustified enrichment. In this view, the Civil Code should be referred to that reflects the nature of the obligation involved in the sphere of statutory bar.

Duty to release unjustified enrichment is owed principally by the party who obtained it. Therefore, it is the party whose assets have increased at the cost of another or the party whose assets got rid of liabilities upon performance of the obligation by the aggrieved party, who is obliged to release unjustified enrichment. If it is a natural person who is due to release unjustified enrichment, the duty mentioned is passed upon his/her death to his/her heirs, but with restrictions under the Civil Code (i.e., only up to the amount of the inherited estate).

The party entitled to demand the giving up of the unjustified enrichment is principally the one at whose expense the unjustified enrichment was obtained. Also, the right to demand the giving up of unjustified enrichment is passed on to the natural person's heirs because these are not property rights restricted to the person of creditor.

The duty to give up unjustified enrichment is based on the principle of full natural restitution. The Civil Code stipulates that everything that was obtained through an unjustified enrichment must be given up. Only if it is not quite possible, especially because the enrichment involved acts, monetary compensation at the usual amount must be provided. The expression 'especially', used in law, allows for a broader interpretation of the prerequisite, when it is not 'quite possible' to release what was unjustifiably obtained, and this is not restricted merely to the cases when performance comprised acts. In considering whether releasing and returning unjustified enrichment is 'quite possible', both subjective and objective aspects must be taken into account, as well as the economic aspects and all consequences of natural restitution of both of the party owing and of the party entitled.

For the extent of duty to release unjustified enrichment, the moment when it was obtained is decisive. Therefore, it is of no significance if, in the meantime and before claiming the right to unjustified enrichment release, its value decreased or was consumed, destroyed or passed over to another person. The state before obtaining unjustified enrichment is to be reinstated through monetary compensation. Thus, the provisions of the Civil Code should be interpreted in relation to the value of the unjustified enrichment obtained.

The bone fide receiver of unjust enrichment shall give up all he/she has acquired but, at the most, up to the limit to which enrichment persists when the law is applied. If he/she has misappropriated the subject matter of unjust enrichment for payment he/she will have a choice either to provide a monetary compensation or to give up what he/she earned. If the bona fide receiver misappropriated the thing without payment the impoverished person has only right to compensation from the dishonest acquirer of the thing. If the enriched person has acquired the subject matter of enrichment bona fide or without his/her consent and the thing cannot be easily given up he/she is not bound to provide compensation unless this state was obviously against good manners.

If the party that had obtained unjustified enrichment did not act bona fide, he/she is bound to also release the benefit obtained from it. Therefore, it should be concluded from the stipulation mentioned that the duty to release involves not only a duty to release the benefit in fact obtained, but also the benefit that the impoverished person might have had but has not obtained. Lack of bona fide is not presumed, but it must be proved by the party claiming the release of benefits on this ground. There is an important provision of the Civil Code constituting the right of the owing party to recovery of the necessary costs incurred on the thing he/she releases to the party entitled. This right pertains to this party regardless of whether he/she acted bona fide or not when obtaining unjustified enrichment. It may only be recovery of costs usefully incurred that objectively added value to the thing, and these costs were necessary or indispensable for keeping the substance or function of the thing.

The bona fide principle is further significant in the view of securing debt satisfying of the party entitled on unjustified enrichment release. Under the stipulation quoted, if the person obtaining unjustified enrichment did not act bone fide, the court may rule that the right to unjustified enrichment release may be also satisfied from the things he/she obtained from unjustified enrichment, including the instances when they are not subject to judgment enforcement (execution) under the Civil Procedure rules. The provision stated applies only if the duty to release unjustified enrichment is realized by monetary compensation, that is, when it is impossible to release what was unjustifiably obtained in natural form.

Imposing the duty to release unjustified enrichment therefore aims at reparations, that is, remedy for economically and legally unfounded property transfers and restoration of the impaired principle of equivalent performance. Thus, the institute of unjustified enrichment by its specific nature contributes to protection of ownership rights as well as of other property rights of natural or legal persons.

§2. Agency without Mandate (*Negotiorum Gestio*) and Using a Thing for the Benefit of Another Person

161. An agency without a mandate is procurement of other person's matter without the procurer having a mandate or any other authorization to act. The consequences differ, depending on whether the agent without mandate was averting a pending damage or whether he/she saved another person's thing from inevitable loss or destruction, or whether he/she procured another matter.

The significant elements are procurement of a matter (the matter being another person's matter), lack of mandate or other authorization and acting for another's benefit.

The agency is based on the promise that other person's matter may be interfered with only if he/she consents to it, or if it is allowed by law.

Interference in another person's matter (principal) is allowed by law only in case of pending damage; in other instances, the person who wishes to procure other person's matter must inform him/her and wait for his/her consent.

Fundamental rights and obligations:

(a) in averting a pending danger, the person whose matter has been procured (principal) is bound to reimburse the necessary costs to the agent even though the agent was not responsible for failure of the result;
(b) when saving another person's thing the person is entitled to adequate remuneration, which is one-tenth of the price at the most, and compensation of purposefully expended costs;
(c) in other instances, if the agent acted without a mandate, he/she is entitled to recovery of costs by which the person, in the interest of which the agent acted, eventually benefited. The agent has this right only if the matter was procured for the predominant benefit of another person.

If an agent is not entitled to reimbursement of the costs incurred, he/she is entitled to take, if possible, what he/she has procured at his/her cost. The agent is obliged to conclude the act, to render an account report, and to hand over all that he/she has obtained to the person for whom he/she has procured the matter.

If an agent interferes in another person's matter otherwise than in averting pending damage, he/she is liable for the damage occurred, and within this, he/she is also liable for accidents, unless it occurred without his/her interference. An agent is equally liable if interfering in another person's matters against his/her express will.

If someone uses someone else's thing for the benefit of another person without intending to procure someone else's matter and if it is not possible to achieve retrieval of that thing its owner may claim compensation from that person for the value the thing had at the time of the use, even if no profit has been achieved.

If someone had expenses for another person who was obliged to have those expenses himself/herself has right to claim compensation.

If a thing was given up in distress in order to avert larger damage everyone who had benefit from that will provide the aggrieved person with proportional compensation.

Selected Bibliography

Eliáš, K. a kol., Nový občanský zákoník s aktualizovanou důvodovou zprávou. Ostrava: Sagit, 2012, 1119 s., ISBN 978-80-7208-922-2 (Eliáš, K. et al., *The New Civil Code with an Updated Explanatory Report*. Ostrava: Sagit, 2012, 1119 p., ISBN 978-80-7208-922-2).

Bejček, J. Smluvní svoboda a ochrana slabšího obchodníka. 1. vyd. Brno: Masarykova univerzita, 2016, 516 s. (Bejček, J., *The Contractual Freedom and the Protection of Weaker Business*. 1st Edition, Brno: Masaryk University, 2016, 516 p.)

Hurdík, J. 'The System of Consumer Law on Its Way to Integration into the System of Private Law'. In *Perspectives for European Consumer Law. Towards a Directive on Consumer Rights and Beyond,* edited by Schulte-Nölke, H.-Tichý, L. Munich: sellier.european law publishers GmbH 2010, ISBN (print) 978-3-86653-131-4, ISBN (eBook) 978-3-86653-878-8.

Hurdík, J. & J. Fiala. 'Czech Private Law at the Beginning of the Third Millennium'. *Legal Studies and Practice Journal* IV (2006): S351–355. Research Revue, Faculty of Law, Masaryk University in Brno, ISSN-1210-9126.

Hurdík, J.-& J. Handlar. 'Konzeption und System von vertraglichen Schuldverhältnissen im Entwurf eines neuen tschechischen Zivilgesetzbuch'. In *Die Reform des Privatrechts in Mittel-und Osteuropa,* edited by J. Lazar. Bratislava-Trnava: Iura edition 2009, S. 330-359, ISBN 978-80-8078-307-5.

Hurdík, J., R. Polčák & T. Smejkalová. *Czech Law in European Regulatory Context.* Wien-München: Verlag Medien und Recht 2009, ISBN 978-3-939438-09-0.

Hurdík, J. & M. Selucká. 'Konsumentenschutz in der Tschechischen Republik'. In *Konsumentenschutz in Zentral und Osteuropa*, edited by R. Welser. Wien: Manzsche Verlags-und Universitätsbuchhandlung, 2010, S. 39-52, ISBN 978-3214-00750-8.

Index

The numbers here refer to paragraph numbers.

Acceptance, 20–21, 41–42
Accession to an obligation, 76–77
Accommodation contract, 124
  for a short term, 124
Account, 142
Actio Pauliana, 80
Administrative contract, 5
Agency, 130–133
  commissionary, 131
Aleatory obligations, 146–149
Annuity, 152
Assignment, 74
Assumption of debt, 75
Auction, 33

Bailment, 134–135
Bank businesses, 142
Bet, *See*: wagering and gaming
Breach of contract, 84, 86
Burden of proof, 38

Capacity, 39, 44
Classification of contracts, 12
Clausula rebus sic stantibus, 41
Collection, 145
Commercial
  agency, 133
Condition, 42–52, 53
Consideration, 22
Compensation
  promise of, 155
Consumer, 98–103
  credit, 118
Credit, 117
  letter of, 144
Custody of securities, 136

Damages, 13, 28, 29, 66, 109
Death, 93
Delay
  of debtor, 28
  of creditor, 29
Deposit, 29, 65, 134–137, 143
Donation, 111
Drafting of contracts, 18
Drawing a lot, 149

Employment, 119
Enrichment without cause, *See*: unjustified
  enrichment
Equality, 6, 18, 59, 71, 72
Error, 39, 45, 49, 51
Exchange, 107

Fair dealing, 17, 39
Fault, 13
Forwarding, 132
Form, 12, 18, 30, 37, 50
Formalities, 24, 50, 59, 62

Gaming, *See*: Wagering and Gaming
Good faith, 17, 39, 86
Gratuitous
  promise, 23
  contract, 23, 116
Guarantee, 4, 5, 12, 109, 133, 148, 151

Hardship, 85
Health care, 113

Immovable, 106–111
Impossibility of performance, 52, 85
Information duties, 39, 100, 113, 118
Injury, 66
Inspection, 157
Instalments, 82

Index

Insurance, 147–148
Interests, 28, 115, 117
Interpretation, 67
Invalidity, 55–66

Land Registry, 104
Lapse of time, 65, 92
Lease, 120
  of a flat and houses, 121
  of an enterprise, 122
  of a means of transport, 123
Legislation (primacy of), 3
Licence, 114
Loan, 115–118
  for consumption, 115
  for use, 116

Mandate, 129
Merger, 96
Mistake, 38, 56, 60
Modification of contract, 25–29
Monetary (performance, obligation, duty), 12, 28

Natural obligation, 24
Negotiorum gestio, 9, 14, 161
Nominate (named) contract, 79
Notary, 37
Notification (of assignment), 78
Nullity, 56

Offer, 20–21, 42

Package tours, 156
Pacta sunt servanda, 26, 86
Pactum de contrahendo, 18
Partnership
  civil, 150
  silent, 151
Payment, 74
Performance, 82
  specific, 84
Place (of payment, of performance), 82
Precarium, 116
Preclusion, 64, 94
Pre-contractual obligation, 39
Prescription, 24, 65
Price, 104
Privity of contract, 69–96
Promise
  public, 23, 154
Proof (burden of), *See* Burden of proof

Property, 15, 66, 77
Public
  contract, 7
  law, 5–7
  tender, 32

Quasi-contract, 14, 158–161

Real rights (in rem), 15
Remission of debt, 90
Representation, 66, 133
Reservation (mental), 23, 38, 48, 51
Resolutive condition, *See* condition
Risk, 112

Sale, 104–111
Seal, 34
Setting of, 12, 87
Settlement, 27, 87
Shipping, 132
Simulation, 38, 51
Solemn contracts, 35
Storage, 137
Suspensive condition, *See* condition

Tenure, 125–127
Termination
  of contract, 81–96
Third party (person), 70–72, 78, 82, 113, 114, 131, 144, 145, 147, 150
Threat, 47
Time of performance, 82
Timesharing, 103
Torts, 13
Transfer
  of rights and duties, 78, 82
  of enterprise, 110–111
  of the contractual position, 78
  property, 106–111
Travel, 156
Trust, 16

Unforeseen (circumstances), 85
Unjustified enrichment, 50, 62, 64, 65, 82, 158–160

Validity, 42–52
Void, voidness, 44, 47, 50, 52, 57, 58
Voidability, 47, 59

Wagering and gaming, 149
Waiver, 89

Warranties, 109
Will, 20–21, 38, 42–51
Withdrawal, 28, 60, 86,
Work, 112

www.ingramcontent.com/pod-product-compliance
Lightning Source LLC
Chambersburg PA
CBHW071345230926
51846CB00002B/451
9789403520933